CORNWALL'S SAINTS

JOANNA MATTINGLY

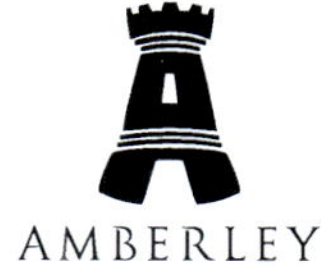

AMBERLEY

First published 2026

Amberley Publishing
The Hill, Stroud
Gloucestershire, GL5 4EP

www.amberley-books.com

ISBN 978 1 3981 2278 9 (print)
ISBN 978 1 3981 2279 6 (ebook)

British Library Cataloguing in Publication Data.
A catalogue record for this book is available from the
British Library.

Typesetting by SJmagic DESIGN SERVICES, India.
Printed in Great Britain.

Appointed GPSR EU Representative:
Easy Access System Europe Oü, 16879218
Address: Mustamäe tee 50, 10621, Tallinn, Estonia
Contact Details: gpsr.requests@easproject.com,
+358 40 500 3575

Contents

Introduction: In search of Cornwall's Lost Saints

It is 1648 and the townspeople of St Austell are ascending and descending the church ladders. They are using pulleys, ropes and chisels to carefully take down the sculpture gallery which was carved nearly 200 years earlier. Plague has brought their esteemed Royalist vicar, Joseph Maye, back to town, his Puritan replacement having run away to a safer living. Visiting the sick daily and burying the dead with full rites, Maye, now in

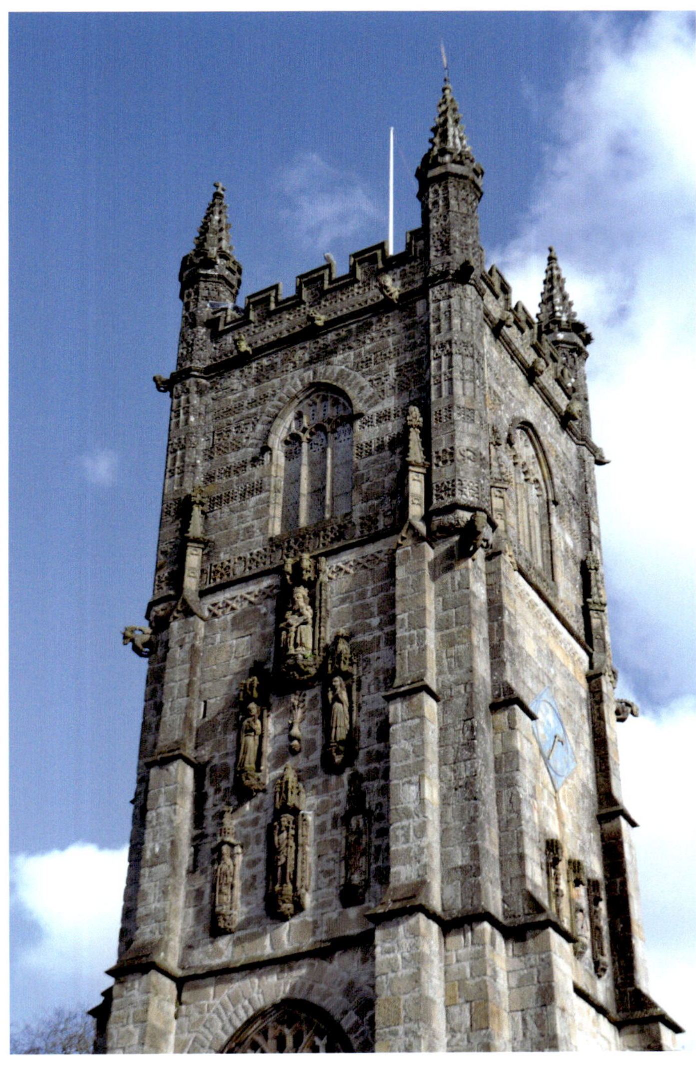

St Austell. Tower sculpture, 1460s. (Photo by Ann Preston-Jones)

his early sixties, miraculously avoids the plague and is considered divinely protected. Very likely he is the organiser of the statue rescue mission. This includes hiding eighteen saints' statues, probably in the homes of Royalist gentry. When Puritanism returns to St Austell, Maye is ejected again. He continues to live in the area or in St Neot parish, where he was also once vicar, supported by loyal parishioners, and dies in 1657 – no one knows where.

Three years after the St Austell 'plague', in August 1651, Parliamentarian soldiers come to St Neot intent on smashing the saints depicted in the church windows. Initially they are foiled by parishioners who form an armed guard; horsemen are dispatched from St Neot to obtain letters of protection, and a coat of lime wash soon diffuses the windows' message. The soldiers vent their anger on the vicarage windows instead.

Reinstatement of St Austell's statues was possible in 1660 when Maye's son, Joseph junior, became vicar there. At St Neot parishioners scraped and washed off the whitewash. Was it due to Joseph Maye's foresight that St Austell and St Neot preserved their art galleries in stone and glass when so many other places did not? Both 'galleries' included local and Brittonic (Celtic) saints, shared with Brittany and Wales.

Cornwall has a rich and diverse collection of saints, and *Cornwall's Saints* will take you on a quest to rediscover this amazing local phenomenon. Why are there so many more

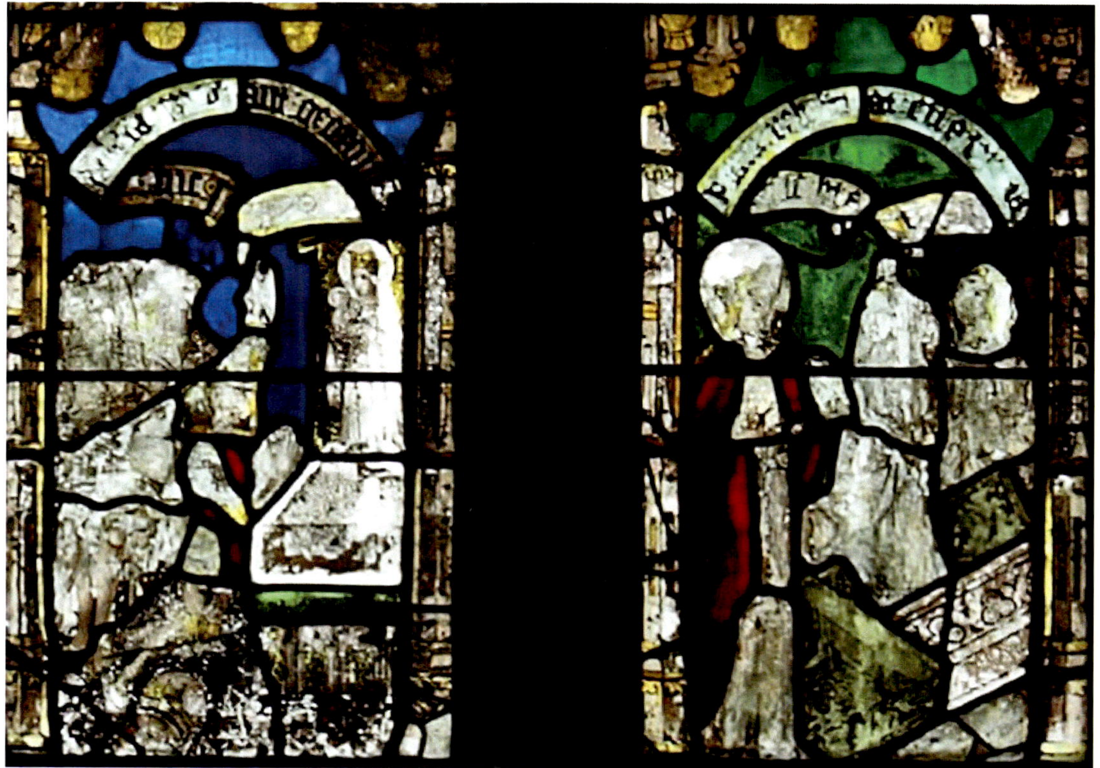

St Neot. St George window details: George prays to Virgin's image and his resurrection, 1500s (p. 65, s7 now n8). (Photo by Eric Berry)

saints here than in Devon or England? Possible reasons include different conversion histories, inclusion of saints' names in place names, and Cornish parishes wanting to have a different saint from their neighbours. At least 142 Brittonic saints representing 187 sites and including 82 saints unique to Cornwall sit alongside international saints canonised in Rome.

Saints were generally people who had led a pious and holy life, including church founders. It was a posthumous honour, with most local saints predating 1050 when Cornwall became part of the diocese of Exeter. Few saints other than Samson, Constantine and Gerent appear in the historic record and they were not approved by Rome. Irish origins were claimed as a matter of prestige, with only Bridget truly being Irish. What matters here is what people believed, not whether saints really lived.

As late as 1359 an unsuccessful attempt was made to create a saint at Whitstone near the Devon border. Its rector, Richard Bovyle, a probable suicide, performed ten post-death miracles before Bishop Grandisson of Exeter stamped out the cult. Grandisson introduced international saints instead of Brittonic ones, like Martin who joined Meriadec at Camborne. A few Cornish parishes lacking saints simply created them from place names: Kenwyn, for instance, meant 'white ridge'. Another phenomenon was that international saints like Agnes could gain a local identity.

Pre-Reformation religion was intercessory in nature, with multiple saints and locations needed. In church, chapel well, field-side shrine or one's own home cross, a saint could be called upon through prayer to mediate with God. Follow-up visits to the saints' holy sites at specified times led to local pilgrimages. Much more common than pilgrimages to St Michael's Mount, Canterbury, Compostela, Rome or Jerusalem, these are largely unrecorded.

Some saints were credited with healing specific illnesses or solving problems. For example, Cadoc, who had a chapel and holy well near Padstow, destroyed internal worms by getting supplicants to drink from his well, while the fifteenth-century Italian housewife saint Sitha helped people find lost keys. There were no fewer than eight plague saints, including Armel, George and Roche. Miracles added to the lustre of a local saint's cult, and local saints might favour local causes. A major aspect of saints' cults was the practice of naming children after saints, and some parish nicknames were derived from saints' names, notably Merryjicks from Meriadec at Camborne.

The focus here will be on saints' cults unique to Cornwall or shared with Wales and Brittany, though three interesting Saxon and Nordic cults also merit consideration. One of them, Sidwell, was a Devon local saint and martyr and Etheldreda of Ely part of her Saxon sisterhood. St Olaf, king of Norway, became mangled as Tooleda (from St Olaf's Day) at Poughill, suggesting a local identity. The international saint Protus similarly became Pratt at Blisland.

International saints' cults including the Trinity and All Saints, and devotions to Jesus and Mary, provide context. During the medieval period saints' cults were obsessed with holy bones and physical relics. This gave rise to artworks from shrines, often shaped as body parts; to images, helped by the late medieval requirement that every church should have an image of its patron saint. In addition, when Royal court commissions lapsed between 1400 and 1509 due to succession disputes and the Wars of the Roses, churches became major patrons of artists and the art galleries of their age.

Saints' names in this book follow the spelling laid down in Nicholas Orme's *The Saints of Cornwall*, not parish names – Maugan rather than Mawgan, for example, unless the parish is being referred to. Written *Lives of* Brittonic saints (see Doble in the bibliography) explain some imagery, the earliest being eighth- and ninth-century *Lives* of Samson and Paul Aurelian. *Lives* of Neot and Petroc start in the tenth and eleventh centuries and there is a *c.* 1300 *Life* of Gwinear by a Breton clerk named Anselm. One of the most enduring legends we shall meet is that of the twenty-four Children of Brychan. This Welsh tale of the twenty-four sons and daughters of King Brychan, who became missionary saints and lived austere lives, was adapted in the twelfth century at Hartland Abbey, Devon. The unknown author included many north Cornish saints' names, with a few male Welsh saints making up the numbers.

Other sources include William of Worcester (1415–*c.* 1482), who visited Cornwall in 1478 and was interested in saints and their burial places, as was John Leland (*c.* 1503–52), who visited on the king's business in 1533, *c.* 1538 and 1542. There are also two surviving sixteenth-century saints' plays in the Cornish language – *Beunans Ke* and *Beunans Meriasek* – covering the *Lives* of the patron saints of Kea and Camborne parishes.

To counteract anti-Catholic tales of Protestant gentlemen like Richard Carew (1525–1620) of Antony, St Endellion-born Catholic and Recusant Nicholas Roscarrock (*c.* 1548–1634) worked on a national survey of saints' *Lives* during his long Cumbrian exile. Early to mid-eighteenth-century gentry or clerical antiquarians like William Hals (1655–1737), Thomas Tonkin (1678–1742) and William Borlase (1696–1772), rector of Ludgvan, were eager to capture local folklore about saints; Hals often garbled such tales, leading to disagreement.

This book is arranged in six chapters, starting with the Cornish landscape and how the medieval Catholic Church appropriated it and populated it with saints' imagery. Chapter 2 focuses on the church interior, using the exceptional Bodmin church accounts and empty niches to show what went where. The remaining chapters are arranged by material and focus on late medieval church features, starting with stone, then wood, metal and embroidery, stained glass and finally the painted walls and panels most recognisable as art today. Places to visit are included at the end.

1. Lost Landscapes of the Saints

Walking in the Footsteps of Saints

Late medieval Cornish people revered the footsteps of their saints. This could involve a meander along a well-defined saint's way or the worship of a saint's foot. A rough granite boulder with the 'footprint' of the Roman Saint Agnes overlain by a larger imprint, perhaps of her tormentor, the Giant Bolster, can still be seen in St Agnes parish. Leading down to the chapel and holy well site of St Agnes, the footprint is near the top of the

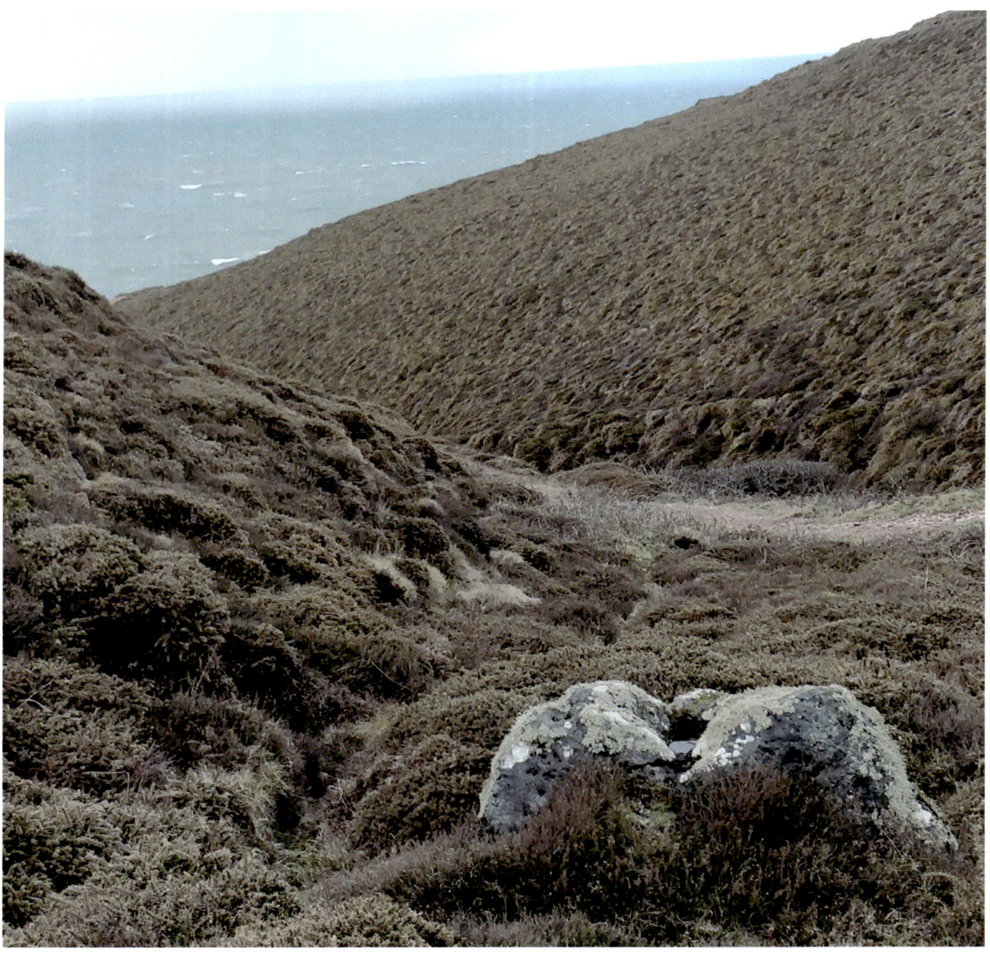

Above and opposite: Chapel Porth. Agnes' footprint and detail. (Photos and sketches by author unless otherwise stated)

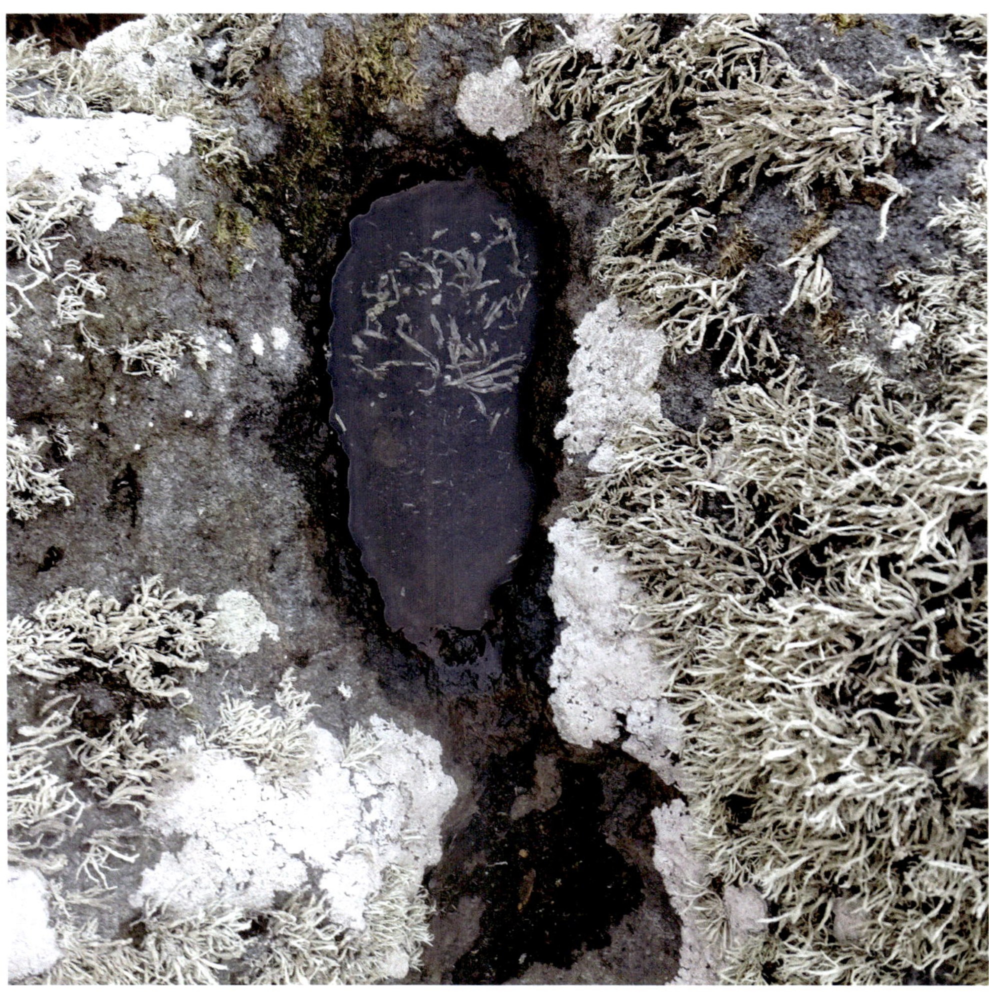

hanging valley above Chapel Porth beach. This footprint can be tested for size, my size eight veering towards the larger imprint of the giant.

'St Michaells foote' was noted in 1655 below Carn Brea in Illogan parish, where the saint had a chapel, but it cannot now be identified. A man-made depression on the highest point of Tintagel Island is today known as King Arthur's footprint, Arthur being the godfather of St Endelient. In Ireland incised footprints were used in early medieval king-making ceremonies, while St Bridget reputedly left fingerprints on rocks.

Before the Reformation, people wanting to see St Ia's foot – presumed to be a foot shrine like St Bridget's sixteenth-century reliquary in the National Museum of Ireland – could go to Troon in Camborne where chapel foundations survive in a wooded valley. The 1534–35 St Ia guild account records an offering of one penny 'to ye seynte ys fotte'; this was enough to buy a small candle. Cornish bequests to saints' foot shrines occur in 1558, when 8*d* was left to Agnes's foot at St Agnes and between 6*d* and 8*d* to Piran's foot at Perranzabuloe.

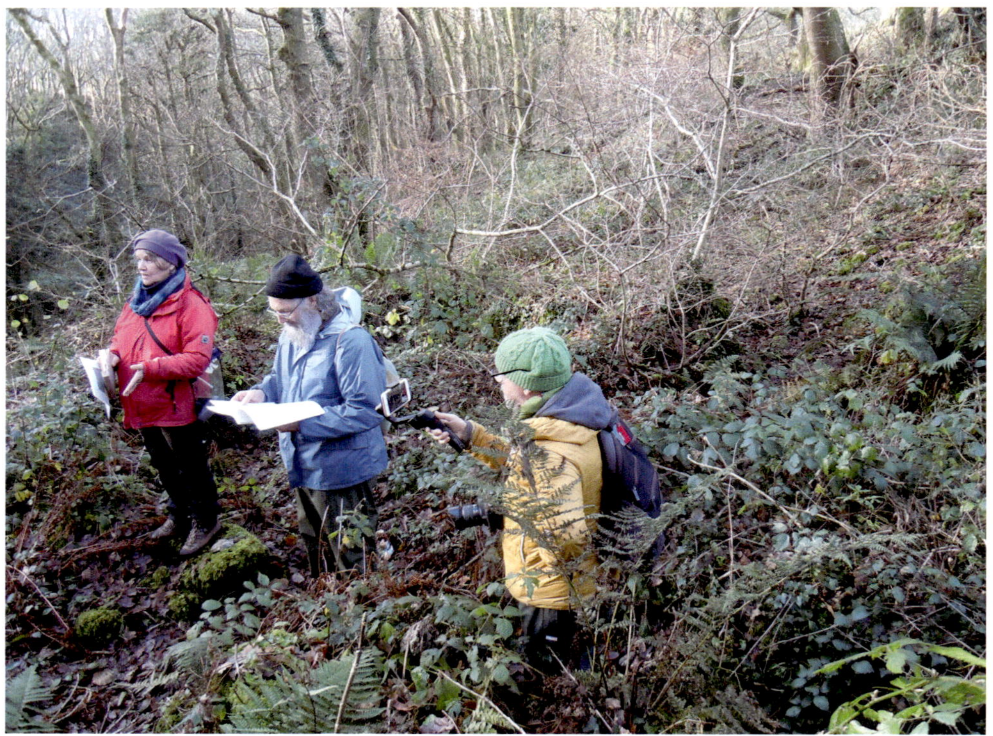

St Ia chapel site, Troon, Camborne.

Ia is most famous as the saint who missed the Cornwall missionary boat. When a magical leaf turned into the Celtic equivalent of a hovercraft, she arrived in Cornwall before Gwinear's party and settled at St Ives.

Holy paths appear in the 884 *Life* of St Paul Aurelian, Roscarrock's early seventeenth-century *Life* of St Dilic (Illick), and Borlase's eighteenth-century St Levan folk tales about St Salamon. Paul Aurelian's path ran along the edge of the sea shore, while Dilic, a child of Brychan, and sister Endelient shared a path between Dilic's chapel and well, in the valley between Pendoggett and Port Gaverne, and the church. This path was greener than any other in the parish, especially after ploughing. In the salt-sprayed parish of St Levan, near Land's End, the green path which St Salamon walked led from his dwelling at Bodellan to his favourite fishing ground at St Levan's Rocks via the churchyard with its saint-split boulder, holy well and chapel. Green grass paths may simply represent local pilgrimage routes.

Holy Trees and Furniture

Trees were associated with holy wells, chapels and occasionally churches, just as holy groves were part of pagan worship, but tall trees are rare in north Cornwall. At St Breward in the early seventeenth century a notable tree was said to mark the site of Breward's martyrdom, and in 1891 a large thorn tree still grew at Chapel Farm well. Further west, Gwinear's staff sprouted at the site of his execution, as Ludewan's may have done; by

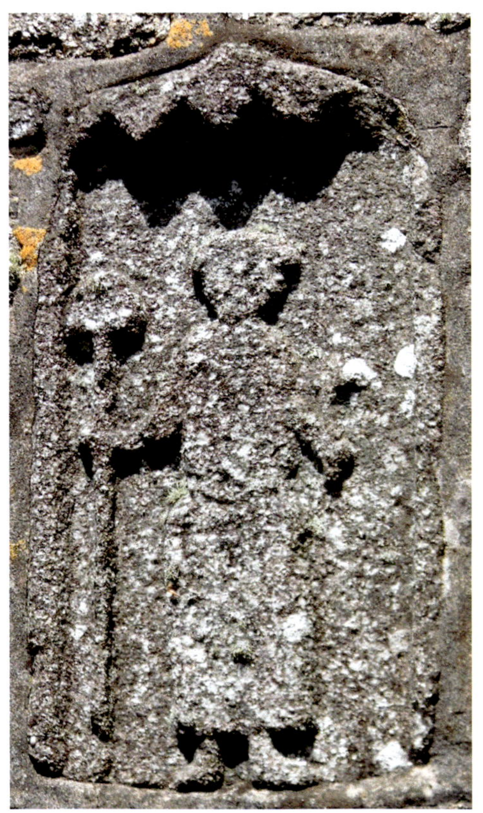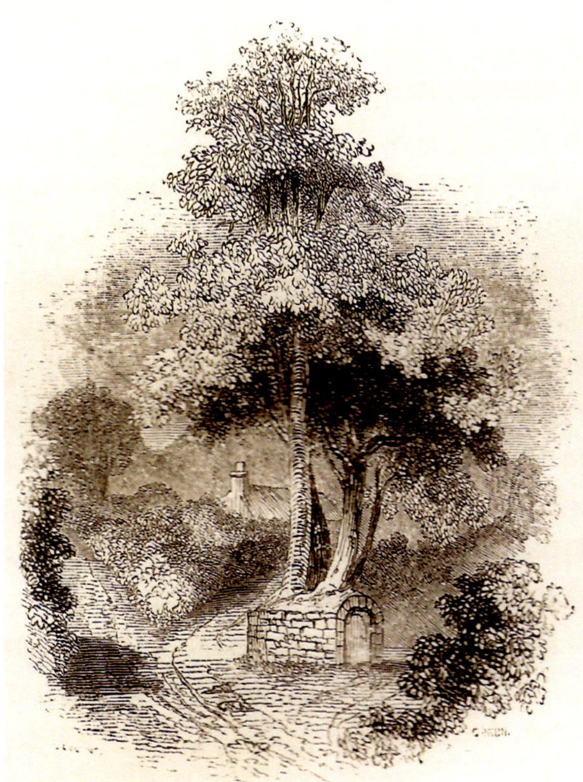

Above left: Ludgvan. Saint with sprouting staff, medieval. (Photo by Andrew Langdon)

Above right: St. Keyne well. (Cyrus Redding, *An Illustrated Itinerary of the County of Cornwall*, 1842, p. 93)

c. 1300 Gwinear's staff was a lofty tree. Withy, oak, elm and ash in 1602 formed the roof of St Keyne well and a whitethorn served the same purpose at Madron chapel fifty years later. Another tree that grew over St Dilic's holy well in St Endellion was for a time protected by dire warnings: when it was felled the perpetrator died soon after. This was also the case more recently with the fig tree growing out of St Newlyn East church.

Saint's chairs were another feature of the Cornish landscape, and two survive. St Germoc's chair at the top of Germoe churchyard takes the form of a small stone-gabled building. The internal arched recesses, which divide the throne-like seat into three, and double-arched entrance are quite unlike any surviving well structure. In 1478 Germoc was called a bishop, but by 1542 he was said to be a king and there is a crowned head over the seat. In the early eighteenth century Tonkin recorded a Cornish saying: '*Germow mahtern, Breage lavethas*', meaning 'Germoc a king, Breage a midwife' – definitely a piece of parish one-upmanship. Germoe was a chapelry of Breage nestling womb-like within the larger mother parish.

The other surviving chair is on the south side of St Michael's Mount and was noted by John Norden (*c.* 1547–1625) and Roscarrock as dangerous, a place of archangel

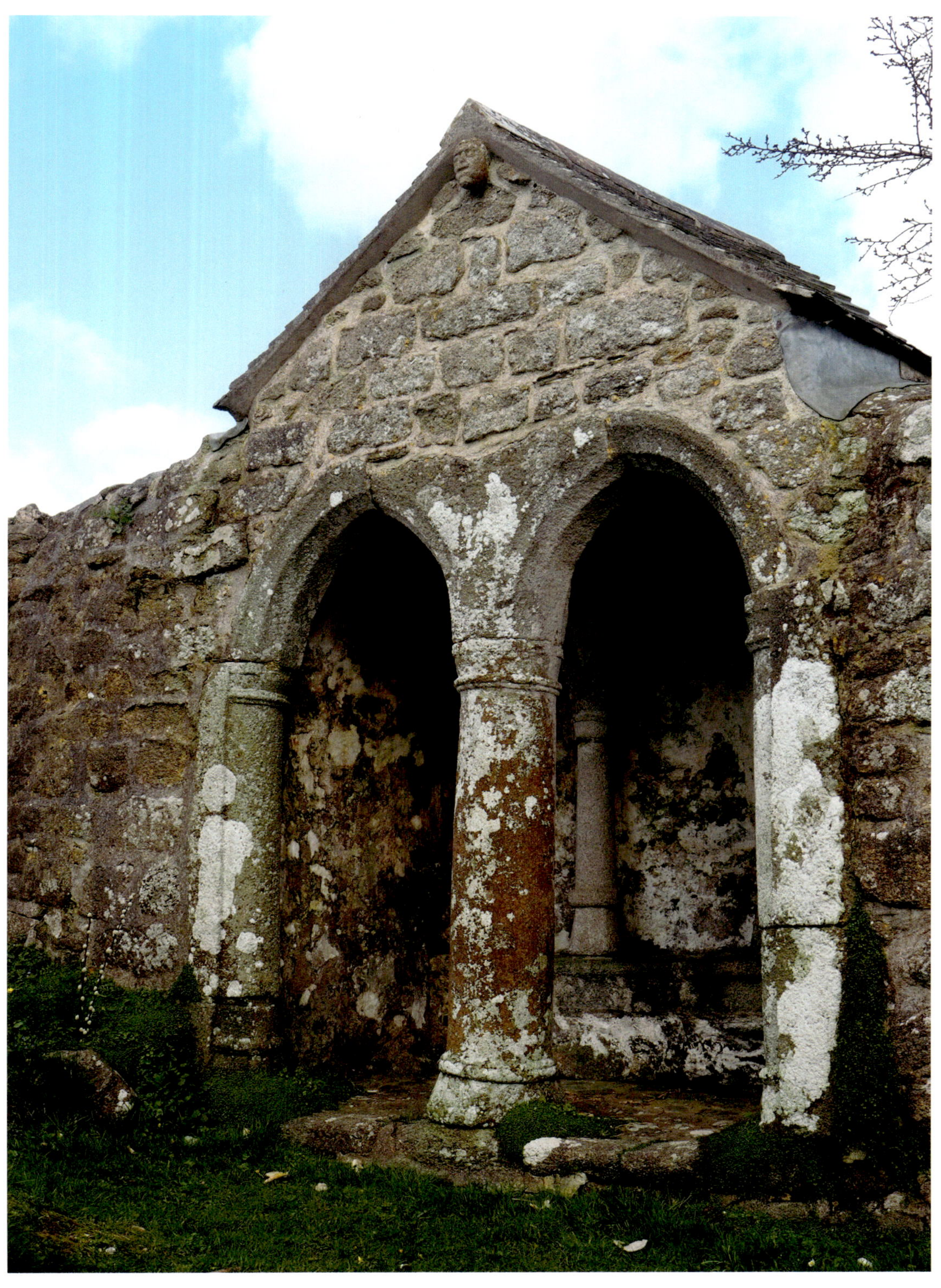

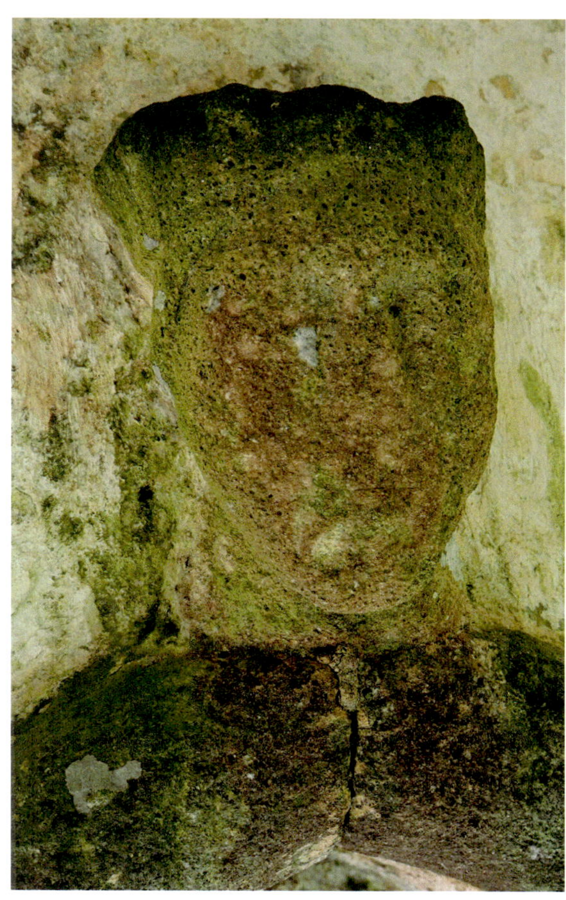

Opposite and right: Germoe. Saint's chair and crowned head, fifteenth century. (Photos by Nina Hocking)

manifestation. At St Mawes in 1542, Maudez had a stone chair in the chapel yard, and a holy well which survives. Modelled on a chair at Maudez's main cult centre on Île Modez in Brittany, his Cornish chair and a painting of him as a seated schoolmaster at St Mawes chapel are both lost.

Saints' beds were not for the use of the saint, but for sick cult followers to sleep on overnight as one stage of a three-part cure. St Salamon's bed at St Levan was actually a large boulder comprising the whole floor of the extant holy well and measuring 5 feet by 5 feet. After bathing in the well water, which was good for eye problems and toothache, Borlase noted in 1748 that visitors were advised to go into this 'chapel' and sleep there three times, with May the best time of year.

A more comfortable bed or green bank was provided at St Madern's chapel and holy well at Madron in Penwith, where miracles were performed up to the Civil War according to Francis Coventry (1598–1680). William Godolphin (1605–63) in 1654 stated that the bed was at the north end of the altar, 'which the parishioners usually repair with turf' annually. The crippled footballer John Trelill slept here under the whitethorn on three occasions in May *c.* 1638 and was cured just in time to enlist as a Royalist soldier and die in battle in 1644 at Lyme Regis.

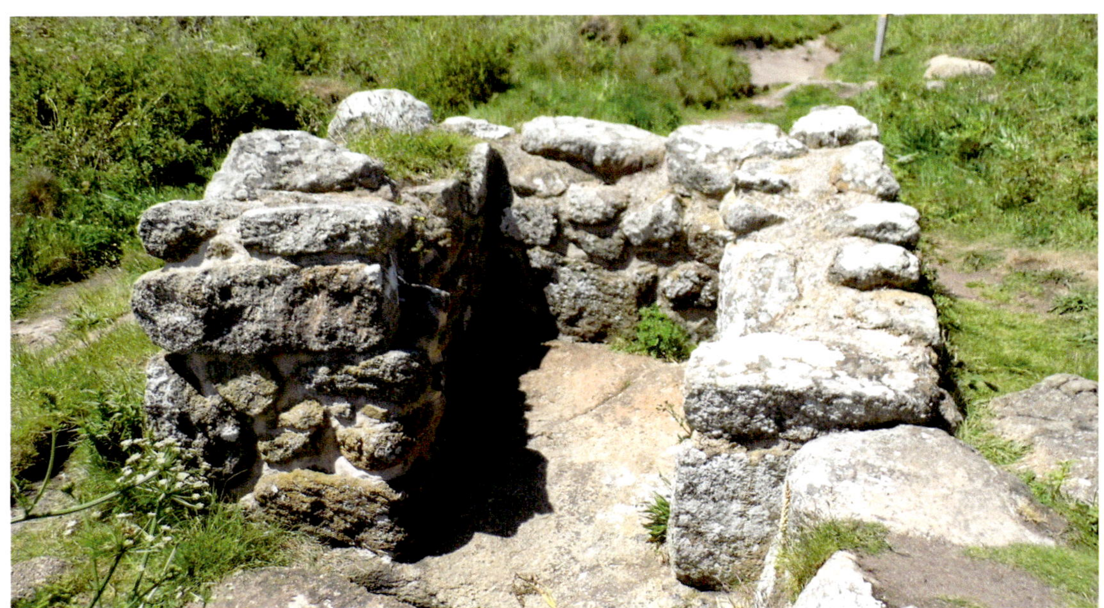

St Levan's Well/bed. (Photo by Andrew Langdon)

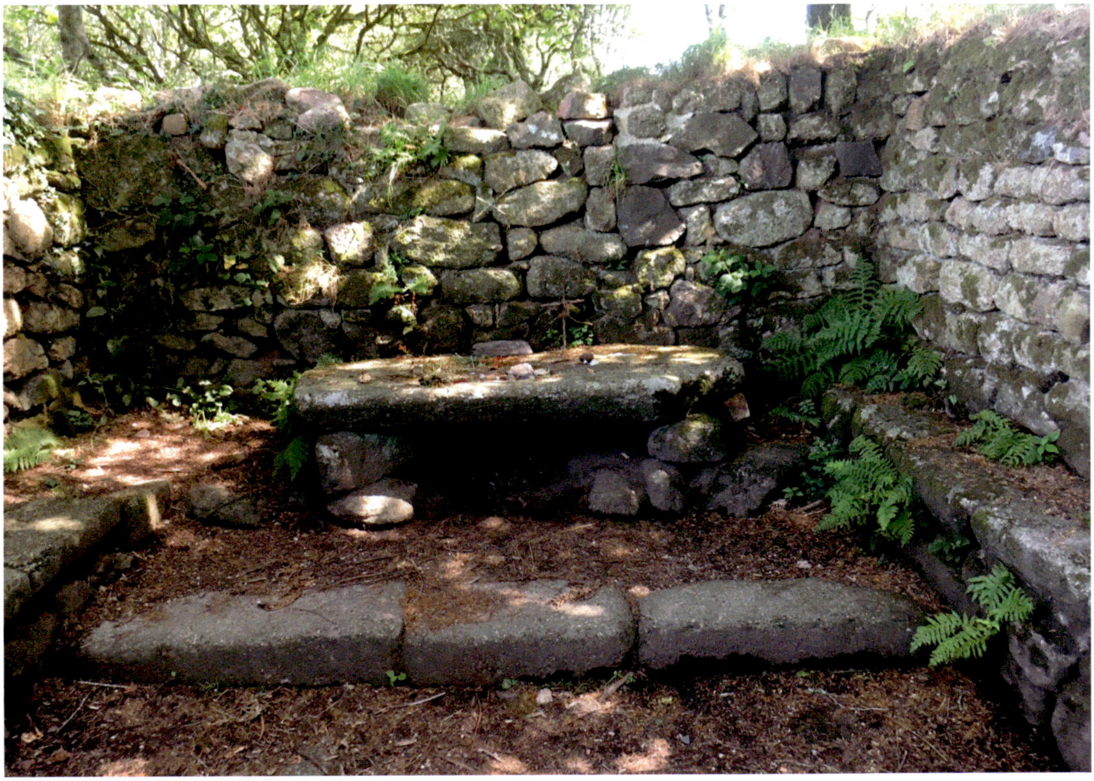

Madron Chapel. (Photo by Ann Preston-Jones)

Chapels and Holy Wells

It is easy to believe in Celtic hermit saints when visiting the holy well and chapel of St Cleder, a son of King Brychan. From the north Cornwall church of St Clether there is a half-mile hike up a valley of rocky outcrops, stunted trees and gorse, and a spongy site at the end. At least twenty and probably thirty or more other Cornish parishes once had chapels, and very often holy wells too, with the same dedication as their parish church. At Gwithian, Lelant and Perranzabuloe chapels may have marked earlier sites, but at St Clether all buildings date from *c.* 1500, rebuilt in 1895–98.

Water from the spring was channelled through the holy well-house – once twice the size – perhaps over the toes of sick pilgrims. It then ran under the chapel wall, over relics and bones behind the altar, and into a reservoir or lower well in the south wall now only accessible by bucket and rope. Madron's roofless chapel also has a now dry reservoir in its south-west corner, while at St Levan water was channelled from the well to the precarious cliff-edge chapel or carried down steps from the well in pitchers like one found in a recent excavation.

Medieval chapels filled the Cornish landscape as Methodist chapels do today, while holy wells belonged to either parish churches or chapels and were not isolated landscape features. Chapels ranged from simple one- or two-cell structures to aisled buildings with towers. They included household, castle, bridge, churchyard, votive, quasi-parochial and urban chapels of ease. Town chapels became parish churches and St Austell, Bodmin, Camborne, Forrabury, St Kew and Probus had churchyard chapels. Landmark chapels,

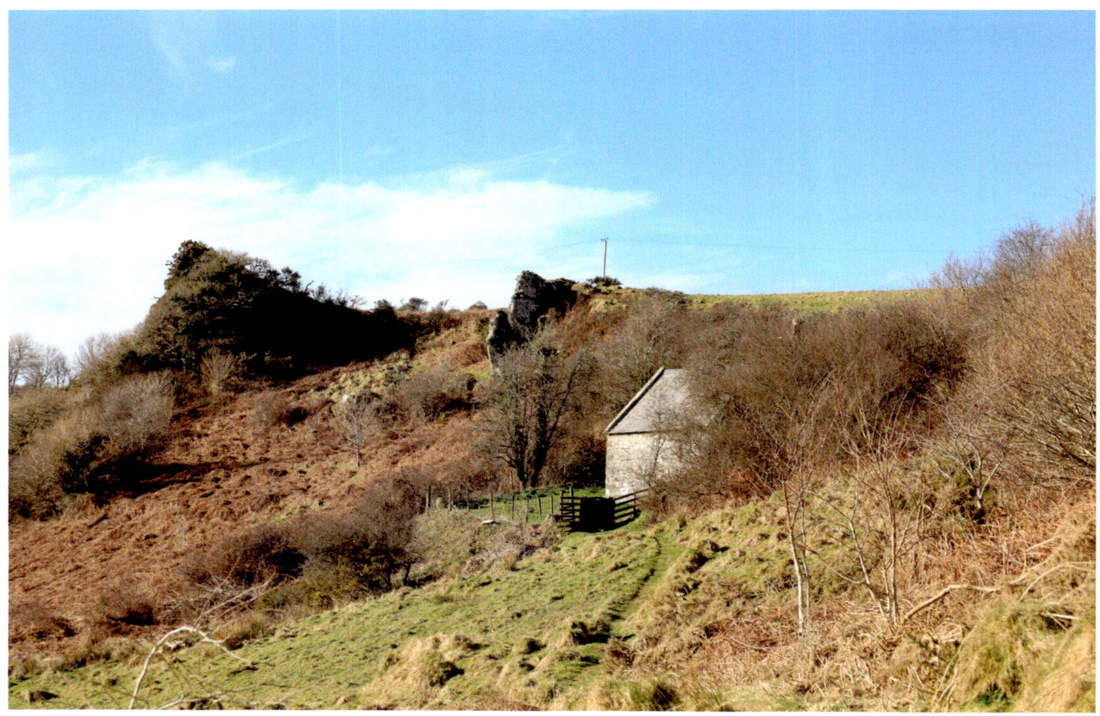

St Clether Chapel, *c.* 1500. (Photo by Alan Stout)

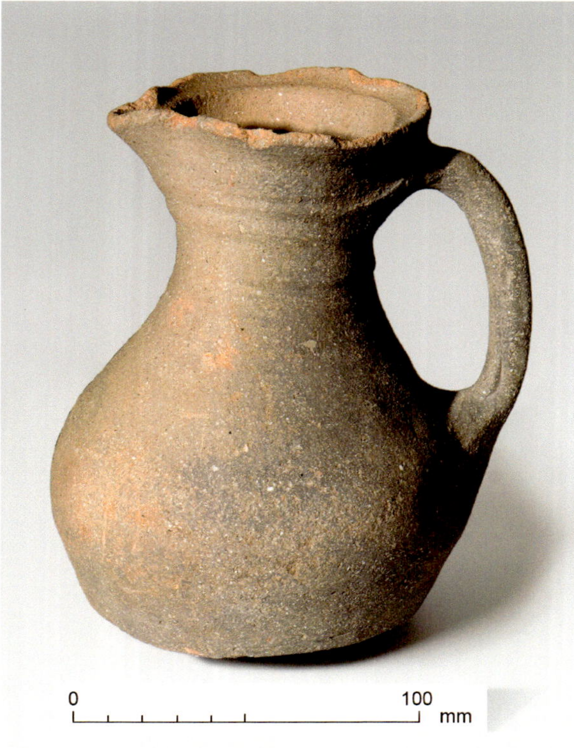

Left: St Levan. Fifteenth-century pitcher from chapel. (Photo by Gary Young, by permission of Cornwall Archaeological Unit)

Below: St Michael's Chapel, Rame Head, medieval.

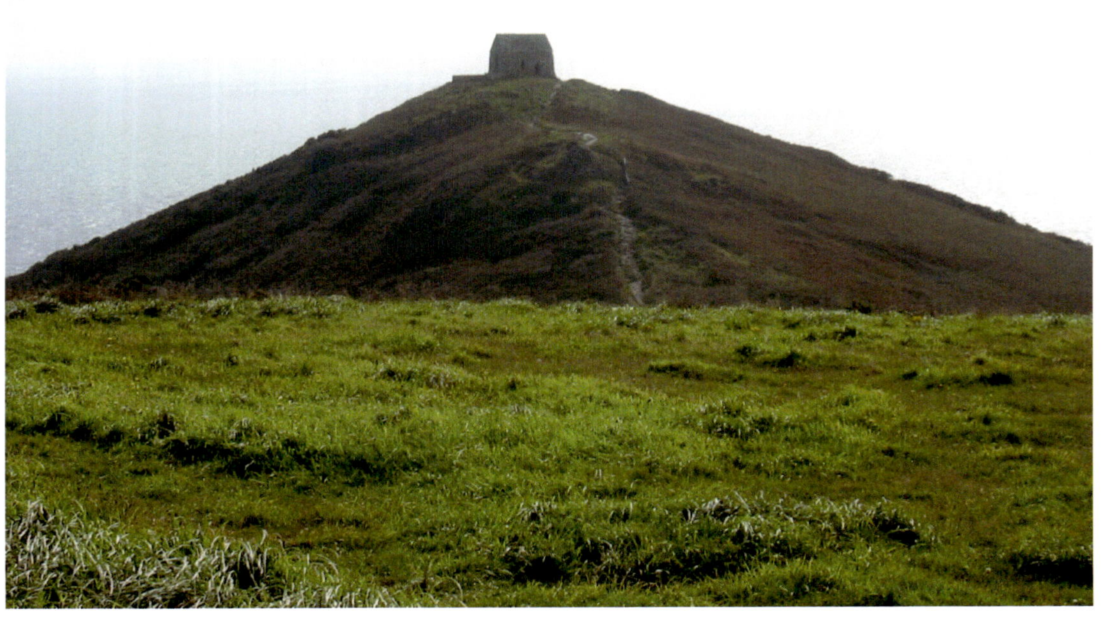

often dedicated to St Michael, were built in the fourteenth and fifteenth centuries on high spots and islands. This may also be when most chapels and wells dedicated to the same saint as the parish church were being built.

Well chapels, like St Cleer, Dupath in St Dominic parish and Menacuddle near St Austell, were smaller than most chapels. Menacuddle is mid- to late fifteenth century in date, while St Cleer and Dupath are early to mid-sixteenth century and may have had separate well-houses. A mason named John Lyswell was documented at Theupath (Dupath) in 1528 and was still living there or nearby in 1544. Arcades on three sides at St Cleer gave greater visitor access than the opposed doors at Menacuddle or the single door at Dupath, but there seems little evidence at St Cleer for the 'bowsening' – the supposedly therapeutic ducking in a pool – of lunatics as described by Carew at Altarnun.

Cornish well-houses are not early structures but contemporary with the great rebuilding of Cornish churches from the mid-fifteenth century to the 1540s. Two slabs enclosed Roseworthy well in Gwinear *c*. 1300, while the *c*. 1400 two-centred arch doorway at St Julian's well, Maker is an 1882 fabrication. Part of the corbel arch supporting the roof and ogee-headed niches are original and replicated at Ruan well, Grade, which has a round-arched entrance typical of *c*. 1500 or later.

Single-cell buildings were suitable for curing sore eyes, a common medieval ailment. According to his play, Kea washed his broken teeth in his (now lost) holy well after a fracas with Teudar, and toothache cures were promoted there. Linkinhorne's holy well

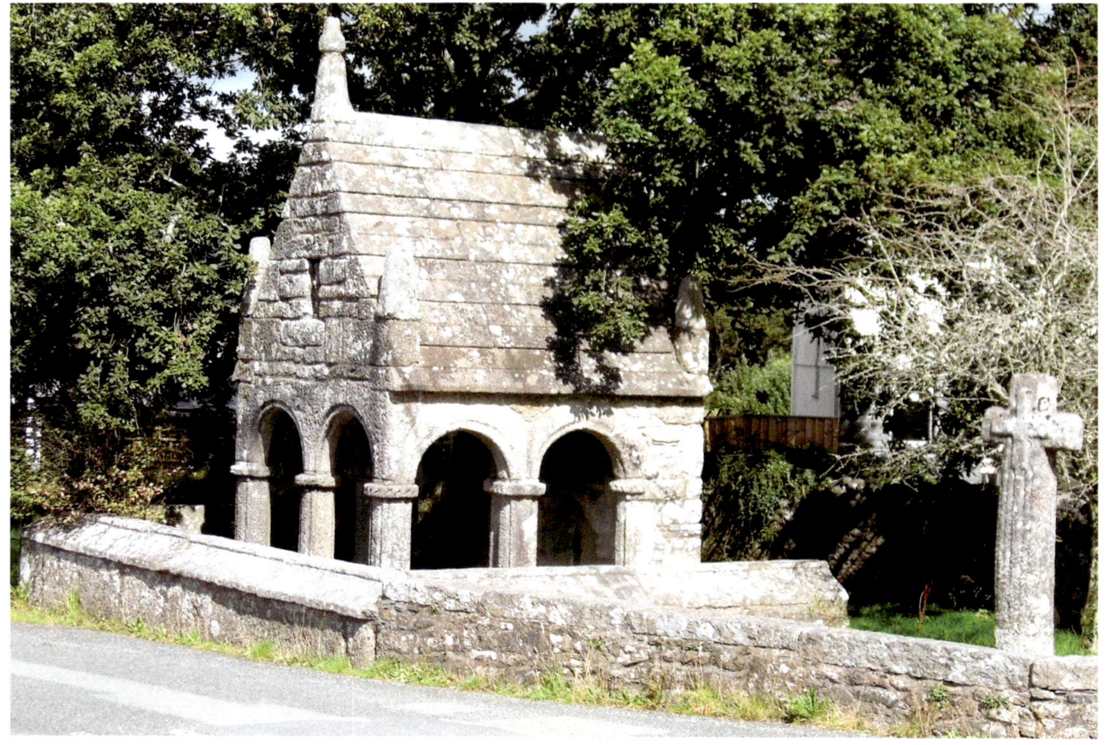

St Cleer Well, early sixteenth century. (Photo by Andrew Langdon)

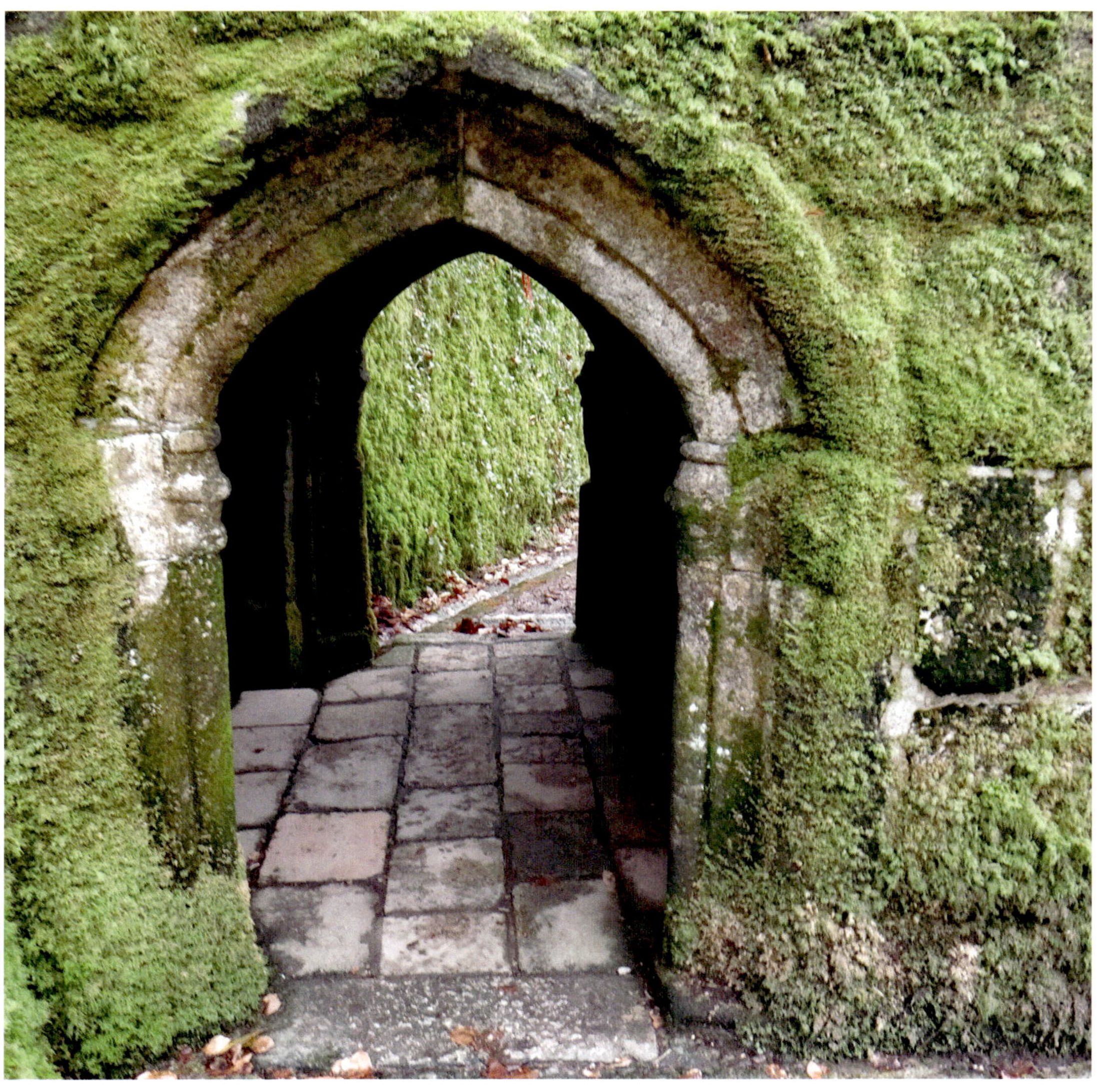

Menacuddle Well, mid-fifteenth century.

of St Melor cured lame cattle and horses; the saint having a silver hand and bronze foot after being deliberately maimed. Porch wells of two-cell type had internal seats at Constantine, Trevornick in Cubert, Trelill in Wendron, and formerly St Agnes, St Clether, Perranzabuloe and Treloy in St Columb Minor parish. The last, dedicated to Petroc, was still operating in 1694, when it cured lame Grace Chinge and Andrew Heddon, who came on horseback from Stratton. Even where no building survives, drought-proof springs were often holy.

There may be 400 holy well sites and more than 750 chapel sites in Cornwall. Niches or brackets show where saints' images once stood, and pinnacles, gable crosses and bell-cotes enhance some. Like Breton chapels today, Cornish ones were richly decorated

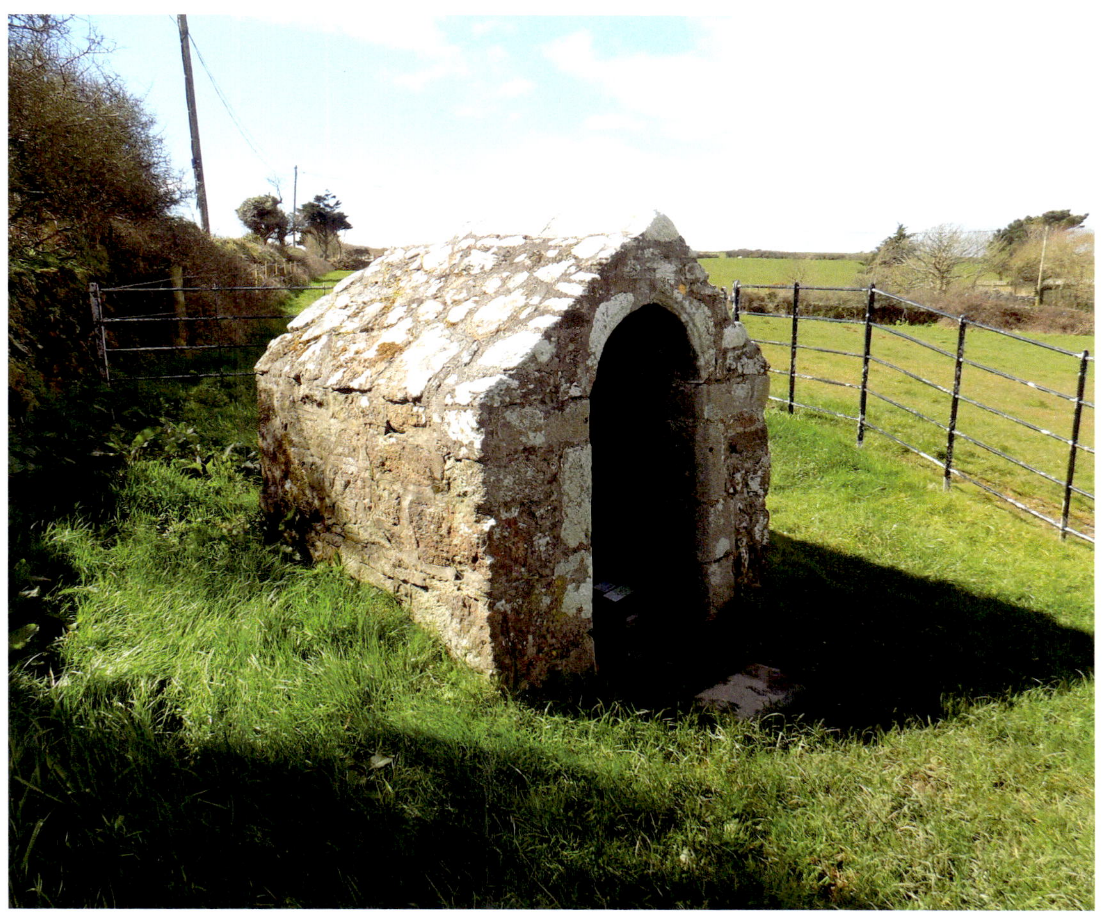

St Ruan's Well, *c.* 1500. (Photo by Ann Preston-Jones)

inside and out, with colourful painted stone or wooden images, carved and painted screens, and stained glass, which survives at Cotehele chapel. A stone statue of saint James from Goldsithney chapel is now in Perranuthnoe church, while the better-carved saint Anthony at Tresillian was found near Merther holy well. It has similarities to the font at Perranzabuloe, and may have come from Merther church. Geometric wall paintings survive *in situ* in the chapel at Erth Barton, St Stephen-by-Saltash, and painted plaster was excavated at St Ia's chapel, Camborne, Lammana by Looe and St Levan chapel.

Even well-houses could have simple red flower stencils and masonry lines painted on their internal walls. St Julian's well, Maker was plastered inside, had two painted statues and a green-and-red-tiled floor in front of the sunken basin. These tiles are similar to Cotehele House chapel and kept Edgcumbe family knees clean when staying at Mount Edgcumbe. Whitewashing would have lightened both well and chapel interiors and made visitors more generous: at Antony in east Cornwall offerings to Christ's and St James's wells in 1549 came to 9*s* and 6*s* 9*d*. To put these sums into a modern context, the former was enough to buy a cow.

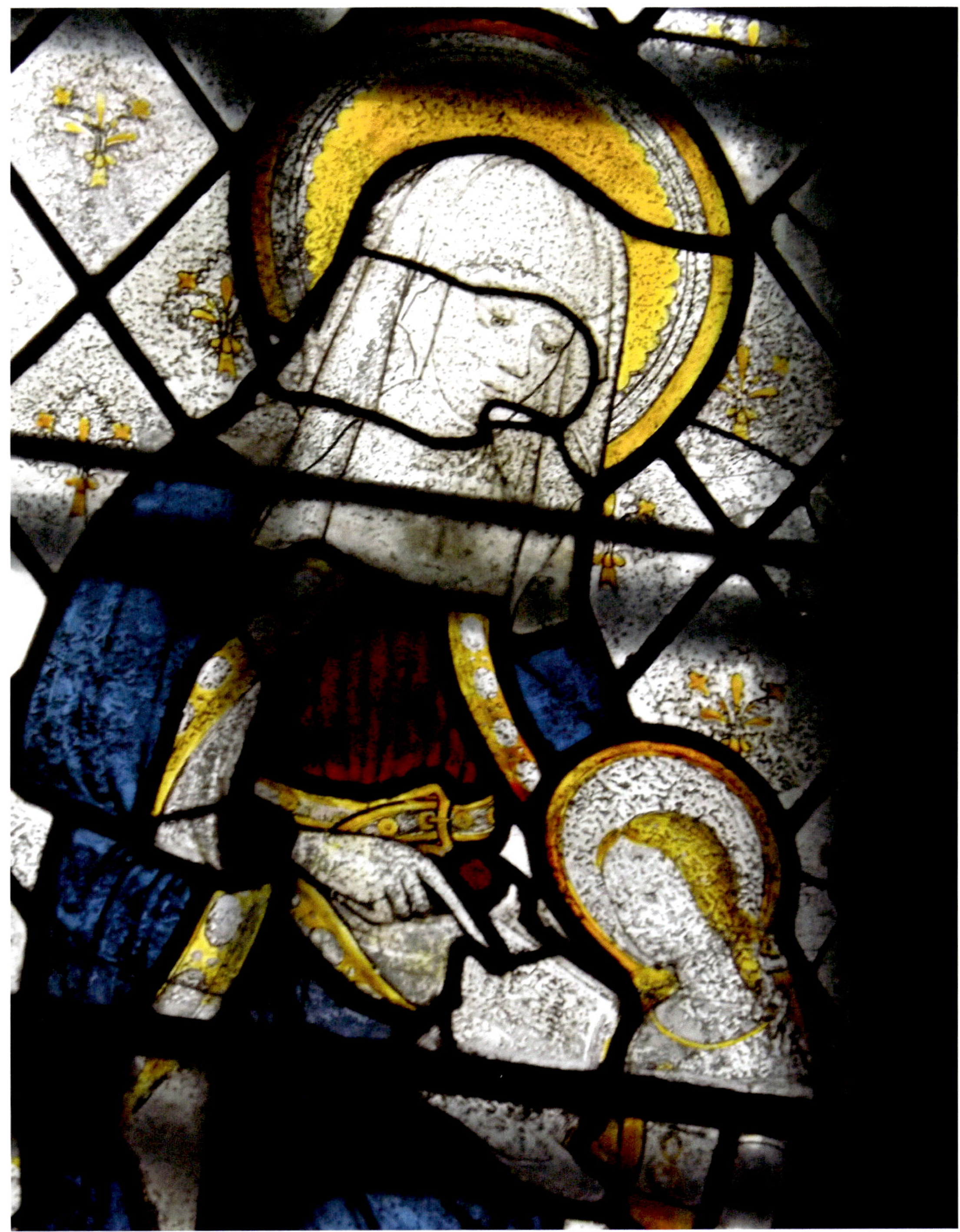

Cotehele House. St Anne teaching the Virgin to read, chapel glass, 1520s. (By kind permission of the National Trust)

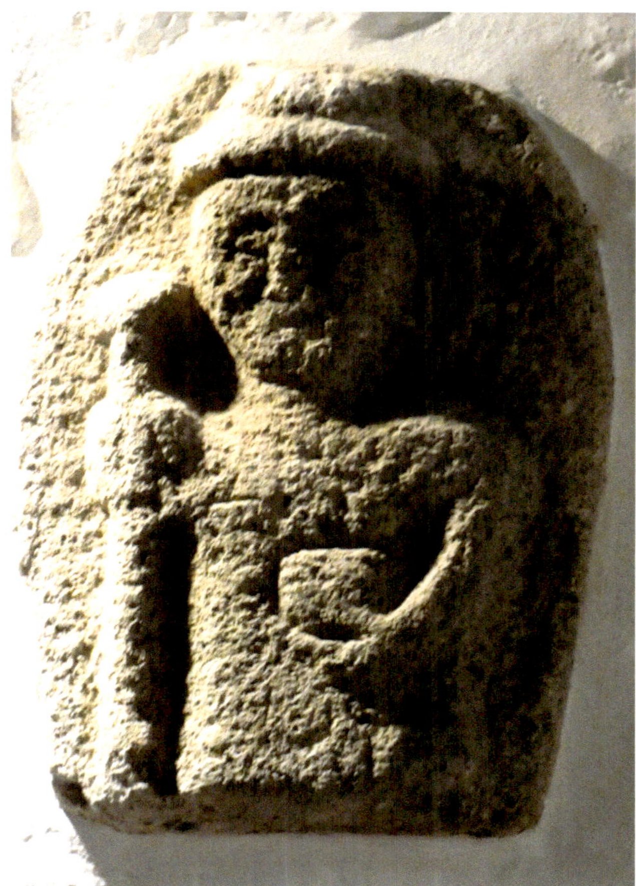 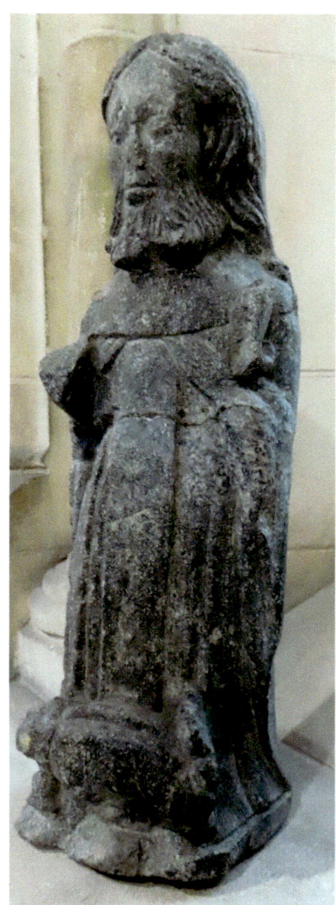

Above left: Perranuthnoe. St James from Goldsithney Chapel, medieval. (Photo by Andrew Langdon)

Above right: Tresillian. St Anthony found near Merther well, fifteenth century. (Photo by Alan Stout)

Landscape Appropriation

Written *Lives* of saints and the plays of Kea and Meriadec, with place-name evidence, show how the Church appropriated the whole landscape. Aetiology, or the mythical explanation of landscape features, in the twelfth century suggested that Petroc's ditches at Bodmin were dug by the saint. At Camborne, Meriadec hid from Teudar under Carrek Veryasek rock, and the same tyrant got stuck in his bath while Kea created one of the larger parishes in Cornwall, including Kenwyn and Truro.

By the early seventeenth century, Lundy Top, a natural chasm in St Minver parish, was explained as the hole the devil made escaping from comb-throwing Menfre, another of Brychan's daughters. When her sister Endelient was dragged to her grave by untamed bullocks, they took her to an early Christian burial ground. At Gwinear, stiles between the church and main settlement were known as the 'twelve apostles' as late as the early nineteenth century, but they were then taken to build the new vicarage.

2. Location, Location –
Saints in Church

Empty Niches

In the ruined church of Merther, a statue niche on the north side of the chancel window once housed a large image of Coan, its unique male patron saint. Known as a martyr with a chapel and holy well, Coan's niche has a canopy, buttressed shafts and a corbelled base. Placing the patron saint to the north of the high altar was common practice with Mary, usually alongside her Lady Chapel, to the south, but at Sheviock, where Mary was the patron saint, there is a single niche on the north side. A pair of early fourteenth-century niches of similar type to Merther and Sheviock can be seen at St Ive, the northern niche once containing Ivo, a Persian bishop, and the church's patron.

These examples highlight where a local saints' image might be found within even quite a small church. We shall now look at how these and other saints' cults manifested themselves at Bodmin in a fully developed and well-documented urban church. Starting in the chancel, where St Petroc and St Mary would have stood, we shall look at chapels to

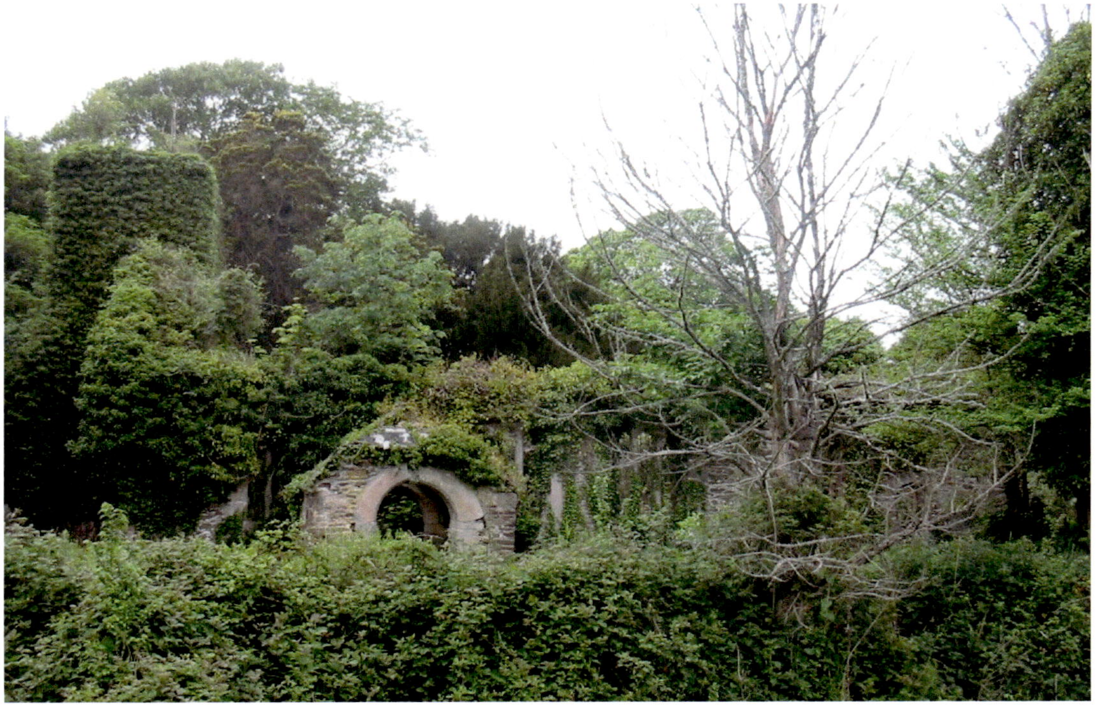

Merther. Ruined church.

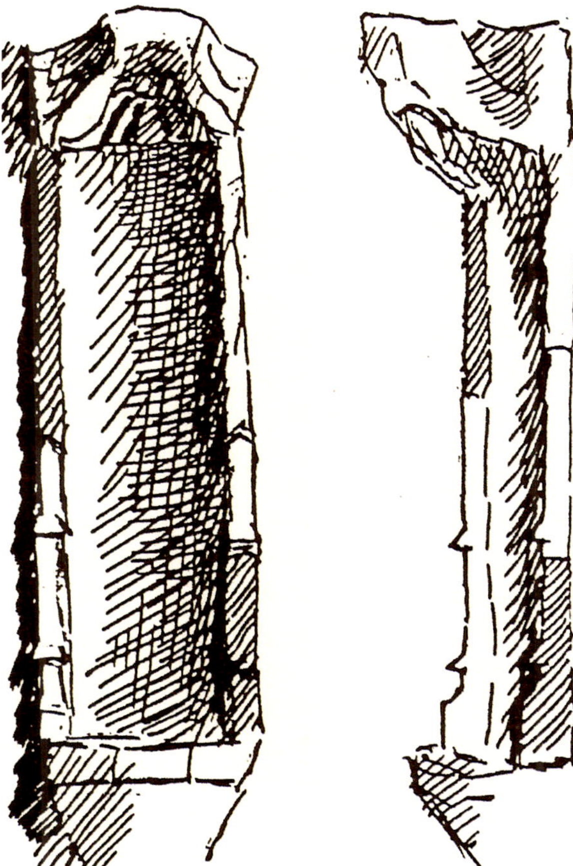

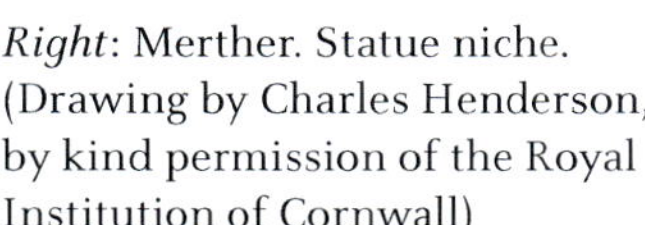

Right: Merther. Statue niche. (Drawing by Charles Henderson, by kind permission of the Royal Institution of Cornwall)

Below: Bodmin. Church plan (Edmund H. Sedding, *Norman Architecture in Cornwall* (London, 1909), opposite p. 22). Image locations: 1=Petroc, 2=Mary, 3=Trinity, 4=Pity of St Gregory, 5=John the Baptist, 6=Martin, 7=Andrew, 8=Henry VI, 9=Rood and Mary, 10=John the Evangelist, 11 apostles? (pageants and histories), 12 Riding George?, 13=Dunstan, 14 = Eloy, 15=Anian, 16=Corpus Christ and several other saints.

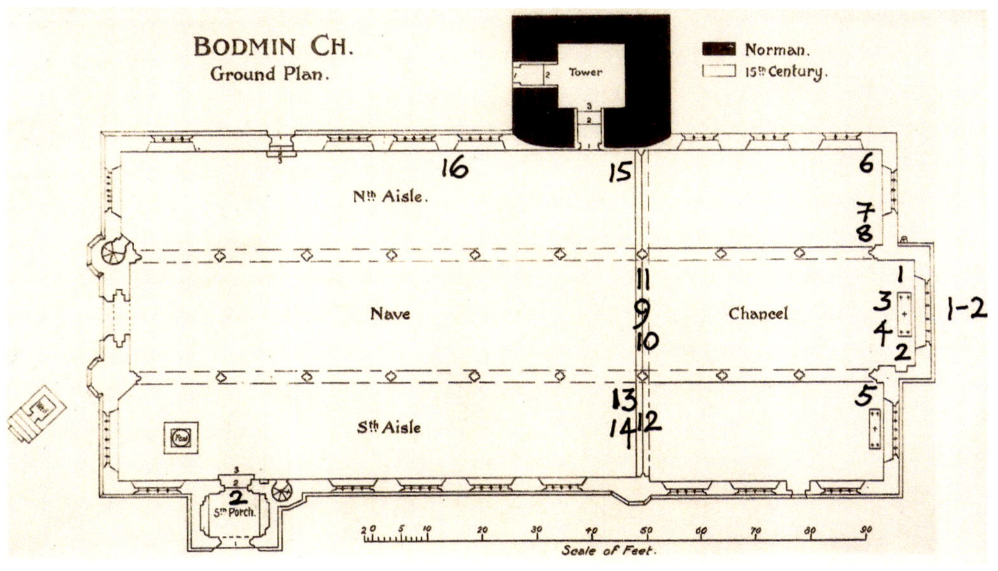

the east (now lost), south and north, then consider the rood loft and its side altars before proceeding west towards the tower. The chapter concludes by considering surviving tombs, reliquaries, Norman north aisles and double chapels as evidence of saints' cults. External niches and corbel brackets will be considered briefly in the next chapter.

Although no statue niches or corbels survive in Bodmin church we know that St Mary's statue on the south side of the chancel had its own guild. By 1539 there was also an image of the Trinity and the pity of St Gregory, perhaps panels from an alabaster reredos, which do not survive. The former Lady Chapel was at the east end of the chancel and served as the chapel of St Petroc's guild. Established for the town's skinners and glovers, this guild was the most important of the five Bodmin trade guilds. Here were further statues of Petroc and Mary, including probably Our Lady of Walsingham (a Virgin and Child).

The Bodmin drapers' guild had their altar and image of St John the Baptist in the new 1469–75 south chapel. Millers and millwrights of St Martin's guild by 1494 split an altar, with St Andrew and the uncanonised King Henry VI, in the early fifteenth-century north chapel. A statue corbel with canopy below in Mabe's north chapel suggests that such double-decker arrangements were not uncommon. Similar north chapels to Bodmin at St Columb Major and St Gluvias have large, elaborate niches on their east walls. At St Columb the large Holy Trinity chapel tabernacles are framed by miniature defaced saints; one held a Trinity and the other St Columb.

The visual focus of worship at Bodmin, as elsewhere by the 1460s, was the rood loft. This high, painted, gilded and canopied structure backed by a wooden tympanum separated the priests' chancel and side chapels from the people's nave and aisles. Such lofts housed the organ and rood or crucifix. At Bodmin there was a residual chancel arch, but by 1500 most Cornish churches had removed chancel arches altogether. Rood lofts offered a wide canvas to both carver and painter, with dadoes, rails, traceried windows, door openings, fan vaulting, canopy beams, wainscoted loft fronts, rood or crucifixion groups, statues and tympani. Apostles were especially popular both below and aloft. Candles burnt constantly in basins in front of the rood and images, vast sums being spent on wax. Stone cresset lamps with four or more holes were common, with survivals at Gwinear, Lewannick, Marhamchurch and St Cadix in St Veep.

As well as rood groups where the crucified Christ was accompanied by Mary and John the Evangelist, statues of St George and the dragon, known as Riding Georges, are documented at St Issey and Stratton. At Stratton the horse was left on the loft when St George was unseated in 1547, but removed the following year. St Issey's 'oss, which locals believed had stood over St George's tomb, escaped Edward VI's bonfires but crumbled to dust in the early eighteenth century. At North Petherwin there was once a wooden image stand with a dragon.

In the south aisle at Bodmin, just outside the rood loft, was the metalworkers' guild altar. This needed two statues, St Dunstan for the goldsmiths and St Eloy for the more numerous blacksmiths. In the same position on the north side of the church was St Anian's altar for the shoemakers' guild. There was also an altar of Corpus Christi in the north aisle, enclosed by wooden screens. Similar free-standing chapels could account for three spiral stairs in St Keverne's north wall. At Lostwithiel, a symbol of Corpus Christi,

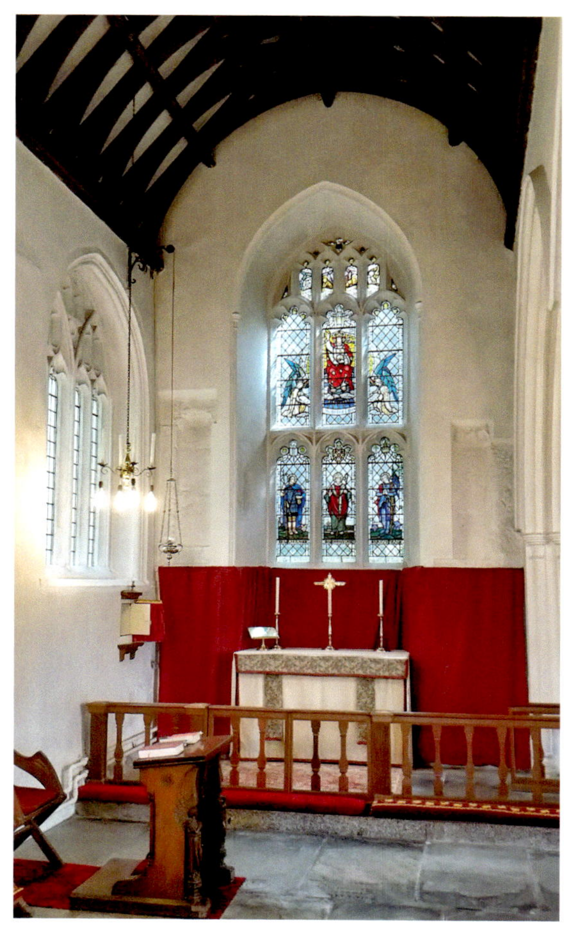

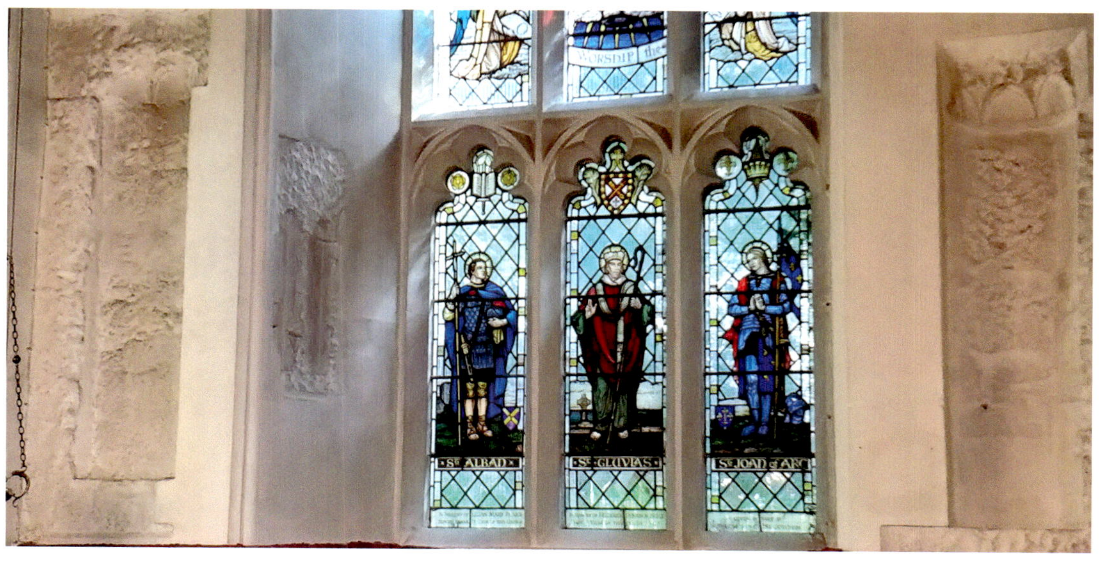

Right and below: St Alban, St Gluvias and Joan of Arc, 1963. North chapel and niches.

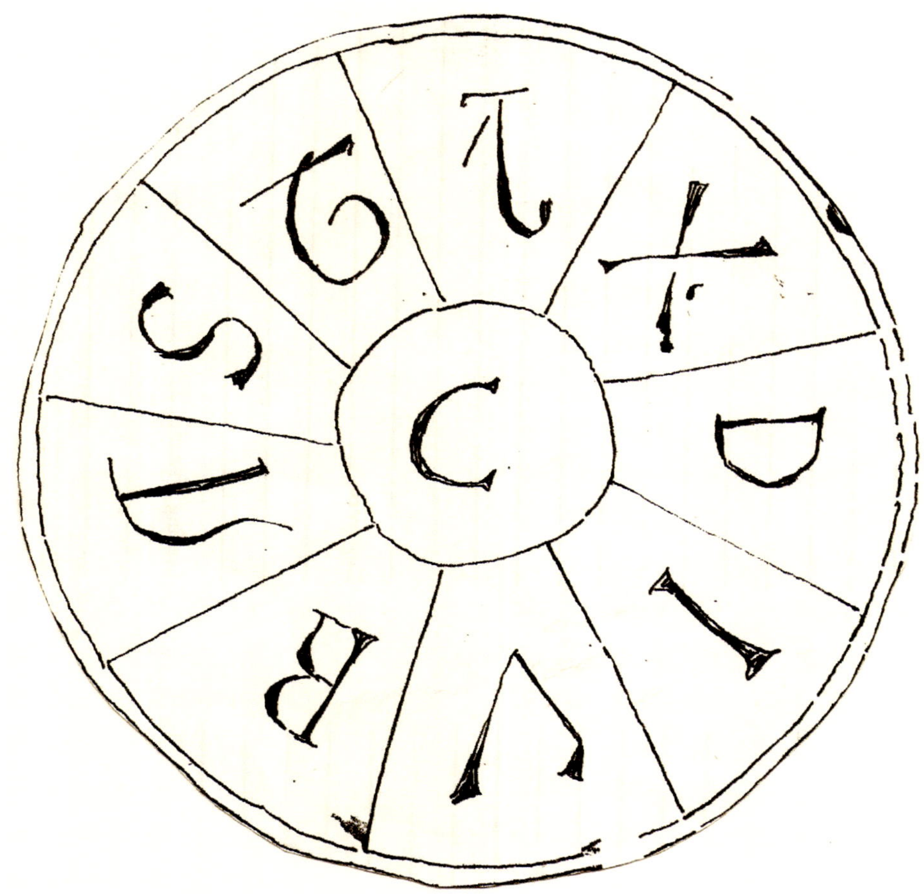

Lostwithiel. Corpus Christi symbol. (Drawing from church records)

the major town guild since the mid-fourteenth century, was once carved on a north aisle pillar where a candle could have illuminated it.

At Bodmin lights burnt before images of Christopher, Clere, James, Jesus, Katherine, Leodegar, Luke, Mary Magdalene, Michael, Peter, Stephen, and the Trinity, most being housed in the nave of the parish church. The south and west faces of Botus Fleming's octagonal pillars are carved with canopies and corbels for three such additional saints. A large grape-and-vine-leaf corbel once supported the north transept altar statue at St Ervan, while a smaller corbel bracket to the west of the north transept entrance at Breage was for St Michael, whose painted image appeared above (see p. 77).

Other areas favoured for saintly decoration in Cornish churches included capitals or corbels of transepts or tower arches, bench-ends and pulpits. Saints sang out from stained glass and wall paintings, with a strong preference for the north side for local ones. Here, opposite the main entrance to the church, there was often a large wall painting of St Christopher, protector against sudden death, while Christ and St Mary could be

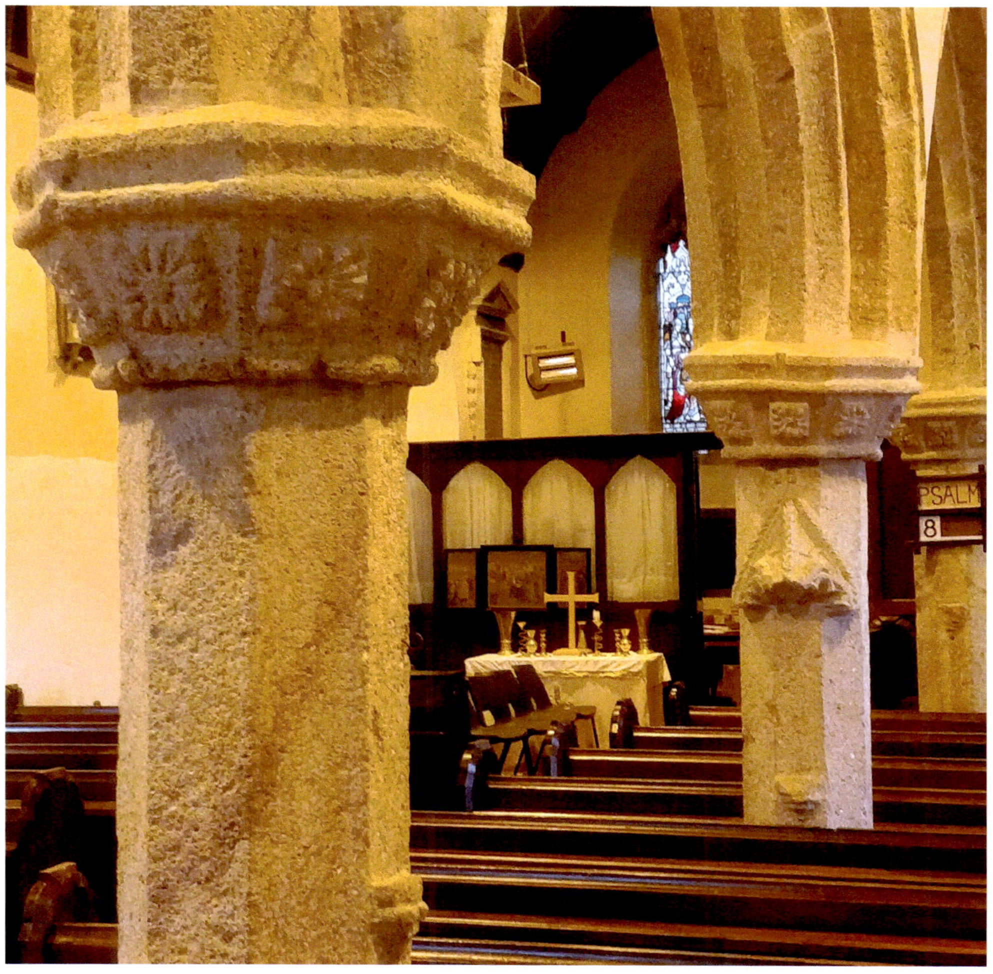

Botus Fleming. North aisle pillars' three statue brackets and canopy, fifteenth century.

anywhere. Church ceilings representing heaven completed the visual sensation, and the blue ceiling at Cullompton in Devon gives a good idea of what Bodmin's catholic parishioners saw when they looked up.

One final embellishment noted in Cornish church inventories was clothing to dress saints' statues on festal days. At Sithney there was a blue silk bonnet for the male saint and at St Michael's Mount the largest silver-gilt Michael had his own small wardrobe. This included two bonnets, one of tinsel satin embroidered with gold and pearl, the other black velvet fringed with gold with additional silver and gilt goldsmith's work. There were also two miniature sets of vestments of cloth of gold, and purple velvet embroidered with Jesus, and a gold chain. A pair of miniature silver slippers probably belonged to the crucified Christ.

Richly embroidered vestments and altar cloths of cloth of gold, silks, satins and woollen cloth added to the colour in Cornish churches. Equally colourful banners and streamers, whether embroidered or painted, were paraded along the church aisles before Mass on Sundays and feast days. Blue was the colour for Advent and Lent and red for martyrs' feast days, with yellow, green, white, purple, tawny and black used, too. Bodmin church had a fine collection of theatre costumes, including a Jesus robe, for its Corpus Christi plays.

Tombs, Shrines and Relics

Documentary references to up to thirty tombs, shrines or bones of saints in Cornish churches and chapels extend from the tenth to the early seventeenth century. Tombs and physical relics were central to pre-Reformation religion and included Barry at Fowey, Endelient at St Endellion, Euny at Lelant, Ildiern at Lansallos, Mertherian at Minster, Nonn at Altarnun, Nunit at Pelynt and Willow at Lanteglos-by-Fowey.

More than 100 Cornish churches, in practice, claimed the corporeal remains of their saint, with pilgrims and worshippers able to touch and kiss the remains. Relics had a value and currency beyond their own church as possession transferred sanctity, legitimacy and spiritual primacy, as well as attracting valuable offerings.

Theft of saints' bones was less common in Cornwall than Saxon East Anglia, and as a result tombs survived in minor Cornish churches and chapels, not just major churches. Padstow lost out to Bodmin Priory on the pretext of Viking raids. St Gennys' head was taken to Launceston Priory, while at St Neot an arm bone was left behind when the rest of his corporeal remains founded St Neots Priory in Huntingdonshire. Rumon was moved, minus his head, from Ruan Lanihorne to Tavistock in Devon during the decades around 1000.

Saint's tombs of fourteenth- and fifteenth-century date survive in Cornwall at Cardinham, St Endellion, St Issey, St Neot and possibly North Hill. Canopies and fragments of possible stone shrines can be seen at Davidstow, St Keverne, Lanteglos-by-Fowey and Phillack. An altar top with chamfered sides and ends but no crosses at Minster might be part of Mertheriana's shrine, where three miracles were performed on 25 July 1477 involving the curing of an insane man, a woman and a girl.

At Cardinham the thirteenth-century shrine of St Meubred also served as the Easter Sepulchre. It comprises a shallow arched recess on the north wall of the chancel supported on each side by demi-columns. Above is a trefoil-headed niche, perhaps intended for an image or candle. The original base of the tomb named Meubred, but it was recycled as sedilia in the late medieval period. At North Hill an ogee-arched recess of early fourteenth-century date served as an Easter Sepulchre and perhaps housed the body of St Terney.

The most monumental surviving tomb fills a whole wall at St Neot church and formerly doubled as the Easter Sepulchre where Christ was ceremonially 'buried' on Good Friday. Of early fourteenth-century date, St Neot's tomb was carved from East Devon (Beer) limestone by a team from Exeter Cathedral. Displaying carved foliate forms and hanging shields like tombs in Ottery St Mary church, Devon, the tomb has a painted back wall. Dust from Neot's tomb was used for cures and sick visitors entered and exited through north doors. When the church was expanded in Perpendicular Gothic style, the tomb was preserved.

St Endellion and St Issey have impressive surviving *c.* 1390s–1430s Catacleuse stone tombs, the stone resembling Purbeck marble or cast iron. Quarried exclusively at

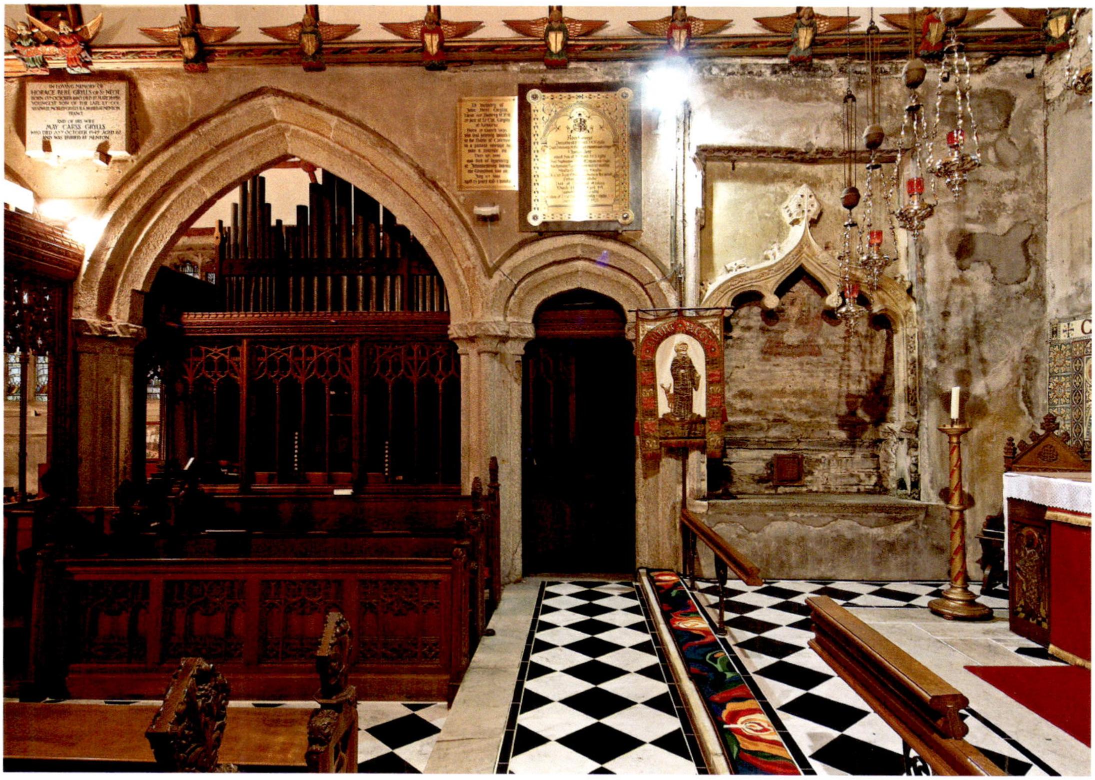

Above: St Neot. Easter sepulchre/
tomb, early fourteenth-century.
(Photo by Eric Berry)

Right: St Endellion. Endellient's
tomb, 1390s–1430s.

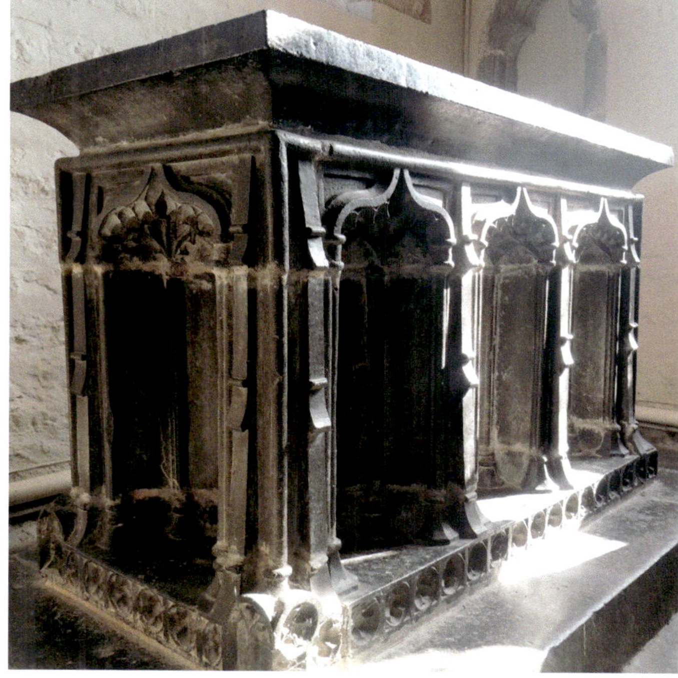

Catacleuse Point near Harlyn in St Merryn parish, Endelient's better-preserved tomb is almost black, though the top stone has been replaced. Its narrow end originally faced west below the first arch of the north aisle, while St Issey's, which is now lacking its front panel, stood against the north wall of the chancel (see pp. 47-8). The other identified Cornish Children of Brychan could have had similar tombs. Nectan's tomb at Hartland in Devon has Catacleuse panels set in a limestone frame and Catacleuse doorways survive at Advent, St Issey and St Mabyn.

At St Endellion the tomb has eight deep niches with flat ogee arches to enable parishioners or pilgrims to get closer to Endelient's remains. Heads, hands, elbows, shoulders, arms, legs, feet or bottoms could be put into these niches, depending on what part needed healing. The St Issey shrine is finer than St Endellion's, but more worn. It has shallower niches and a sculpted band above. At first sight this looks like a row of cut-out paper dolls, but it may well be a depiction of twenty of the Children of Brychan (see pp. 48). Similar kneeling niches to St Endellion can be seen in Lincoln Cathedral at Little St Hugh's tomb shrine and formerly at St William's tomb in York Minster.

The Bodmin casket displayed in that parish church is the most extraordinary survival. Purchased probably in Westminster in 1177, this beautiful casket of ivory, wood and brass, with green and gold bird-and-interlace roundels, may originally have been a Sicilian-made Arab dowry chest. Walter of Coutances, Henry II's ecclesiastical fixer, took the casket to St Méen in Brittany to recover Petroc's bones which had been stolen the previous year. Petroc's head was placed in the casket and other bones put in a larger, purpose-made

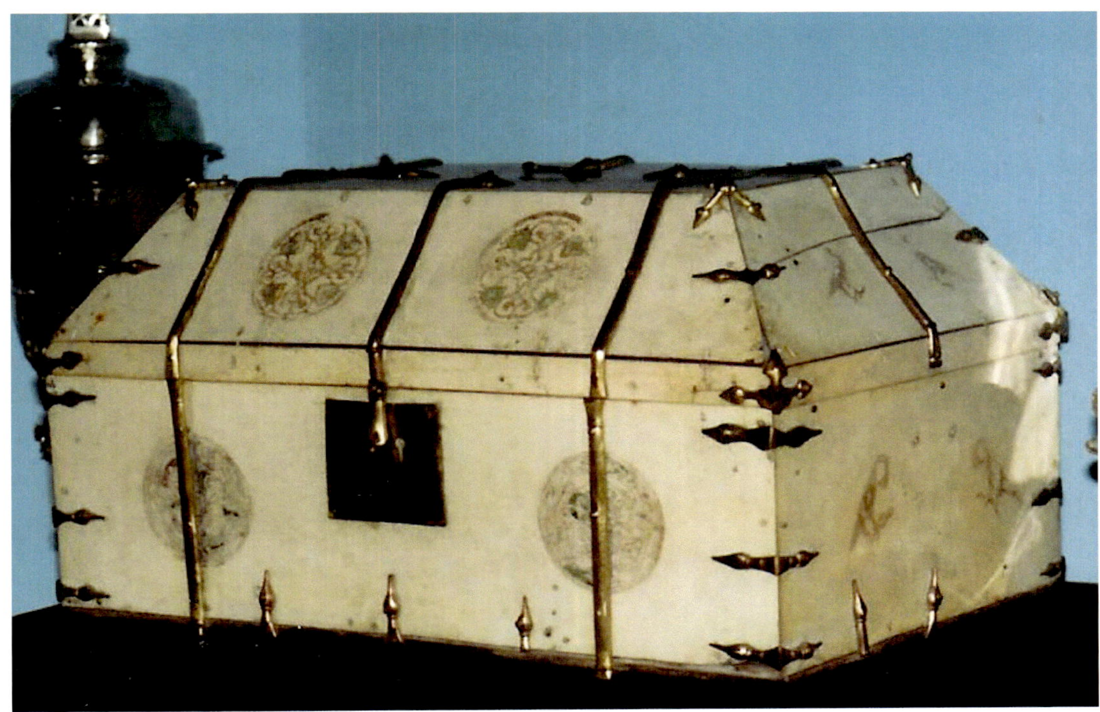

Bodmin casket, late twelfth century.

wooden shrine; a few bones were left as a diplomatic gesture. Back at Bodmin Priory, both shrines were covered with a silk pall given by king Henry II. According to Roscarrock, parishioners of three of Petroc's six Cornish parishes – Bodmin, Little Petherick and Padstow – went in procession on 4 June to Maen Gurta on St Breock downs for a sermon and a feast. From Bodmin this was an arduous 12-mile round trip for casket, priests and parishioners.

In 1548, Liskeard had a silver shrine and St Michael's Mount a box of gilded timber for saint's relics among its silver and gilt shrines. Triangular-headed stone reliquaries or altar pieces depicting crucifixion groups have been identified from St Allen, Bodmin, Breage and St Keverne parishes. It is also possible that one of two skulls found walled up in the chancel at Probus relate to Probus, the patron saint.

Other local saints had contact relics: for example, a bell, staff and King Constantine's ivory hunting horn hung over Petroc's Bodmin shrine. Petroc's hunting horn, sword and bell are depicted on a bench-end at Little Petherick and the bell at St Issey (see Chapter 3). Bits of Petroc including fragments of his clothes were at Exeter, and his spear at Llanbedrog in Wales attracted offerings of £4 per annum in 1535.

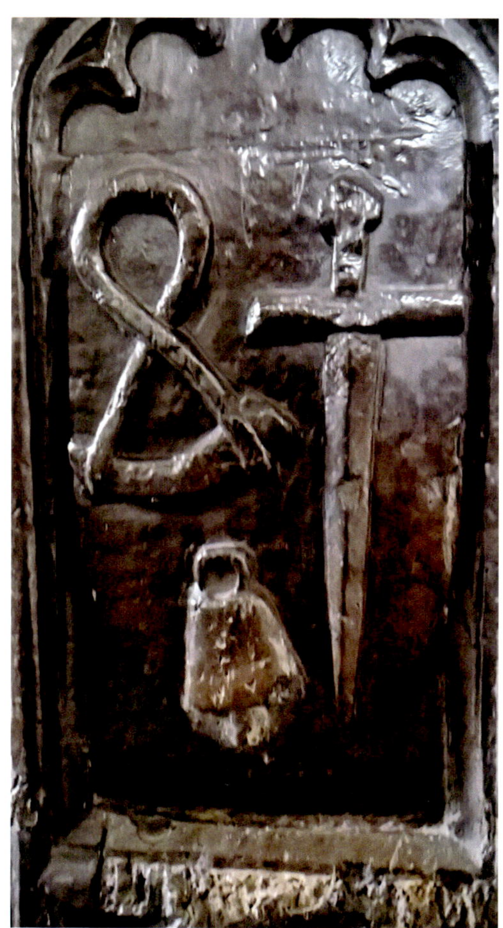

Little Petherick. Petroc's hunting horn, sword and bell, bench-end detail, sixteenth century.

Bodmin church in 1539 claimed to have a thorn from the crown of thorns in a silver-gilt pax. St Michael's Mount claimed two parts of the crucifix, a sword and pair of copper-gilt spurs of Henry VI, and the jawbone of St Apollonia, whom we shall meet again in Chapter 6 and the Epilogue (see p. 88).

Norman North Aisles and Double Chapels

Aisles with Romanesque decoration were most common in larger minster churches or priories, like St Germans, but in Cornwall, single Norman aisles on the north side of the church survive at St Breward, St Buryan, Lelant, Morwenstow and North Petherwin. At St Clether, the Norman aisle may have been on the south side and single aisles probably existed at St Issey, St Just-in-Penwith, Linkinhorne, Pelynt, South Petherwin and St Teath. At Sithney, where documents suggest Sithney's tomb lay, recent excavations found a lack of wall footings on the north side of the nave suggestive of an earlier aisle. Too low and narrow for processions, north aisles perhaps provided a convenient corridor for visitors to saint's tombs.

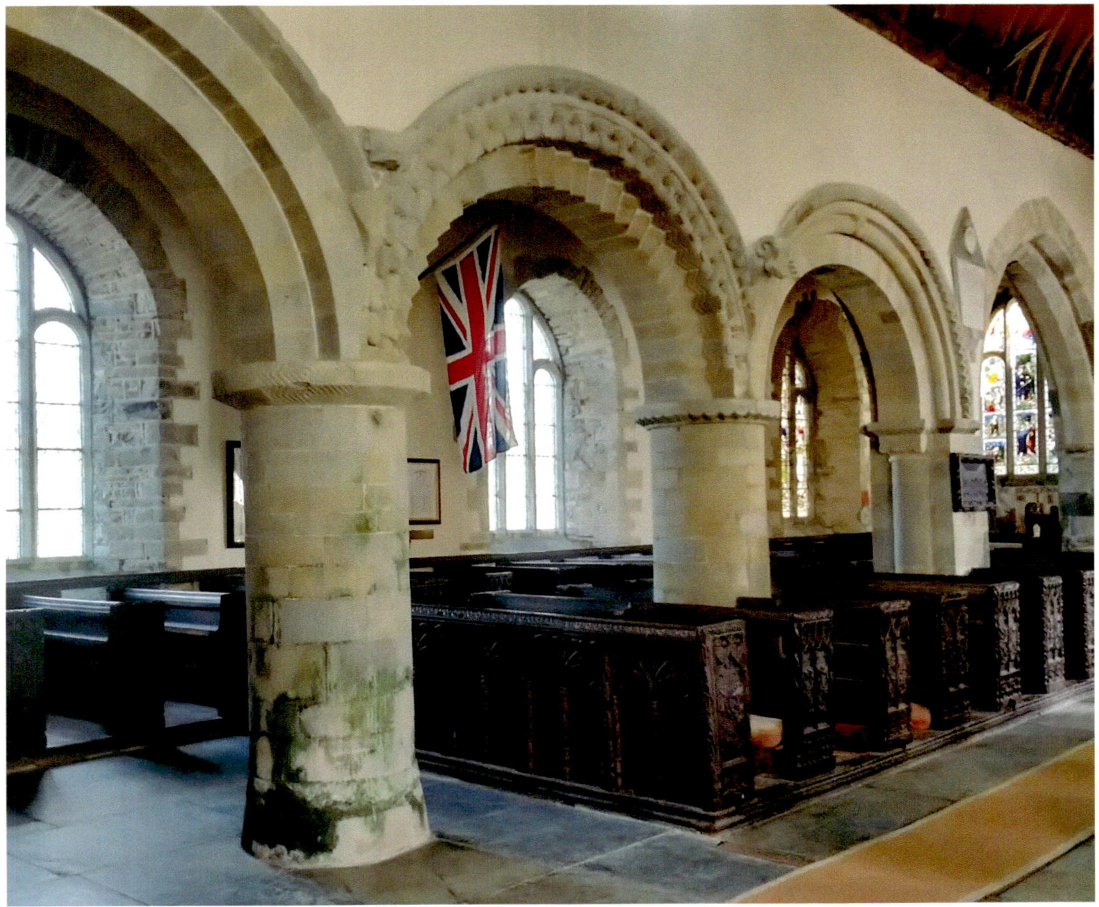

Morwenstow. Norman north aisle widened in the mid-sixteenth century.

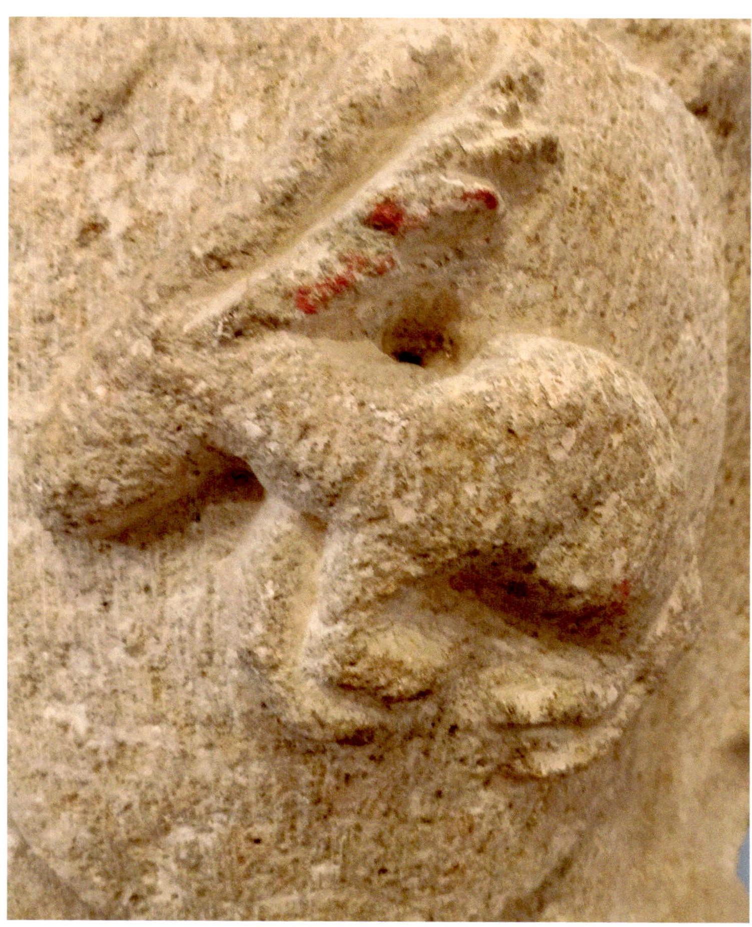

Gwinear. Saint's stag, mid-fifteenth century.

Cornwall has two churches, Constantine and Gwinear, with unusual double chapels on the north side of late fourteenth- to mid-fifteenth-century date. Both honoured important local saints, Constantine a Cornish king and Gwinear a missionary leader. Constantine also appears in the *Life* of St Petroc as a pagan hunter and rich man. Converted to Christianity by Petroc, Constantine's second Cornish cult site was a chapel and holy well in St Merryn parish near Padstow.

At Gwinear an early to mid-fifteenth-century date is likely for its double chapel and guild. A carving of a stag on the south face of a capital of the outer aisle relates to the saint's *Life*. Gwinear was converted to Christianity in Brittany after killing and skinning a stag. A 1920s painting at St Hilary church of St Fingar (Gwinear) by Newlyn artist Harold Harvey shows that, after creating a spring to wash his hands, he was so moved by his own reflection and God's goodness that he became a hermit. Gwinear later appeared to a huntsman in a dream after being massacred. Next day a stag the huntsman was pursuing sought sanctuary where the saint's unburied body lay and the huntsman remembered the dream. He buried the saint and his companions in a Christian manner at the site of the future church.

3. Saints Set in Stone

Stone Saints Outside

Over 150 empty image niches and corbel brackets survive on Cornish church exteriors, most on towers and porches. At Veryan, where the church has no west tower, niches are on the west-end gables instead, but may have come from a chapel in Grampound. There is also a niche at Stithians over the south chapel window which marked the main way to church. With a focus on local saints, we shall start with tower imagery, including decorated corbels, before considering porches, south aisles and east ends. Comparisons will be made with churchyard lantern crosses, covered fully elsewhere, before moving inside.

Single empty statue niches on the west fronts of towers can be found at St Endellion, Jacobstow, Lansallos, Launceston St Mary Magdalene, Stratton and Zennor. Paul church has three empty niches on the west front of its tower, while St Blazey and Week St Mary have south-facing tower niches. Probus's Somerset-style tower has impressive triple niches low down on both north and south sides. At Poughill a niche on the east side of the tower probably held St Olaf, like the partly extant St Nectan, oldest son of King Brychan, at Hartland, Devon. St Austell tower outdoes all with eighteen niches, six on the west and four each on the other sides, all still filled with 1460s statues (see p. 4).

The St Austell west front figures diminish in size from top to bottom with apostles of the smallest size in groups of four on the other tower faces. Although partly countering the perspective from the ground, size and position show the relative importance of each saint. Dominating the hierarchy is a Trinity with dove probably added in paint. Two angels hold four souls in a napkin below. Under this is the Annunciation with Gabriel and St Mary, a restored lily pot between them, and at the bottom Christ, of similar size to the last figures with apostle-sized flanking figures.

These last are local saints: Austell, the original patron saint of the church, and his neighbour Mewan. Austell appears as a long–haired, fork-bearded hermit wearing a cloak over his gown and holding rosary beads and a staff. He is described as a hermit by Leland *c.* 1538, with Mewan shown as a clean-shaven, mitred, short-haired bishop wearing a chasuble, his right hand raised in blessing and left holding a cross staff. Corbels carved with kings' heads, rather than angels, include a horned devil under Austell.

In the eleventh-century Breton *Life* of St Mewan, Austell was his godson and a priest, though the tower carvings make Austell the older man. Roscarrock noted in the early seventeenth century the great friendship between these saints of neighbouring parishes and thought the bishop statue was Austell.

Only one other Cornish church, Mawgan-in-Meneage, still has a local saint on its west front, though there may have been a crowned head at Constantine in a similar position. The Mawgan carving, just above the west window, is small and shows a bishop wearing a mitre and chasuble under a simple 'corrugated' canopy, now rather obscured by lichen.

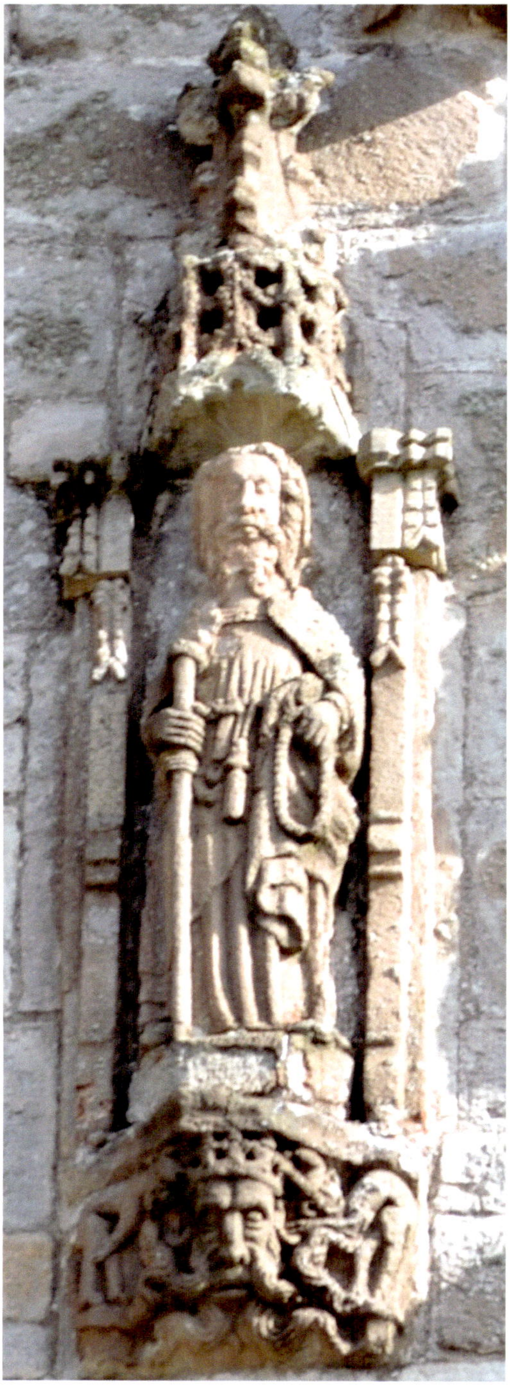

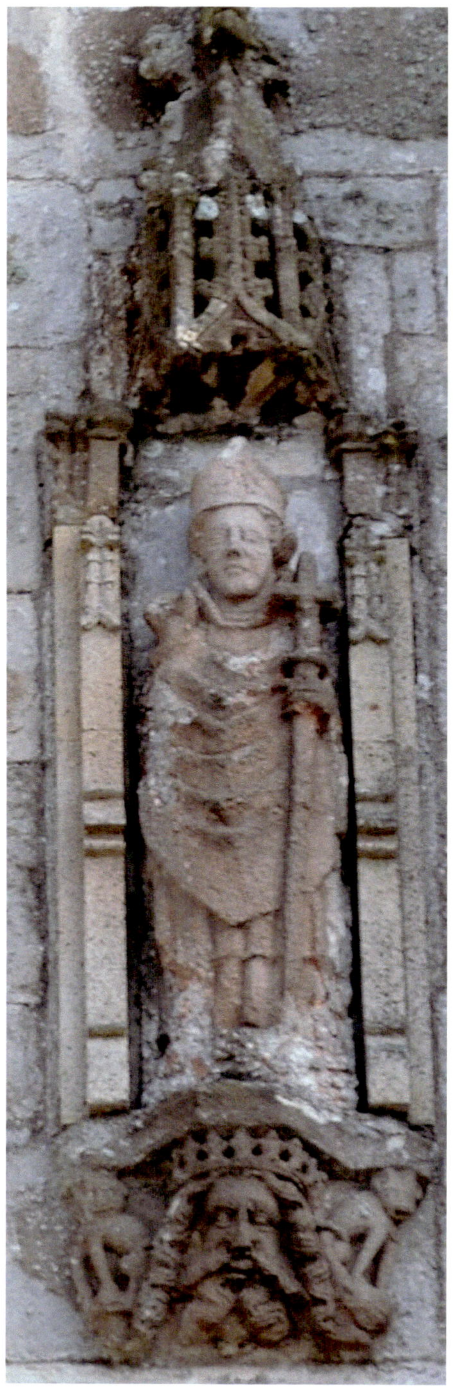

Above left: St Austell. Austell, 1460s. (Photo by Ann Preston-Jones)

Above right: St Austell. Mewan, 1460s. (Photo by Ann Preston-Jones)

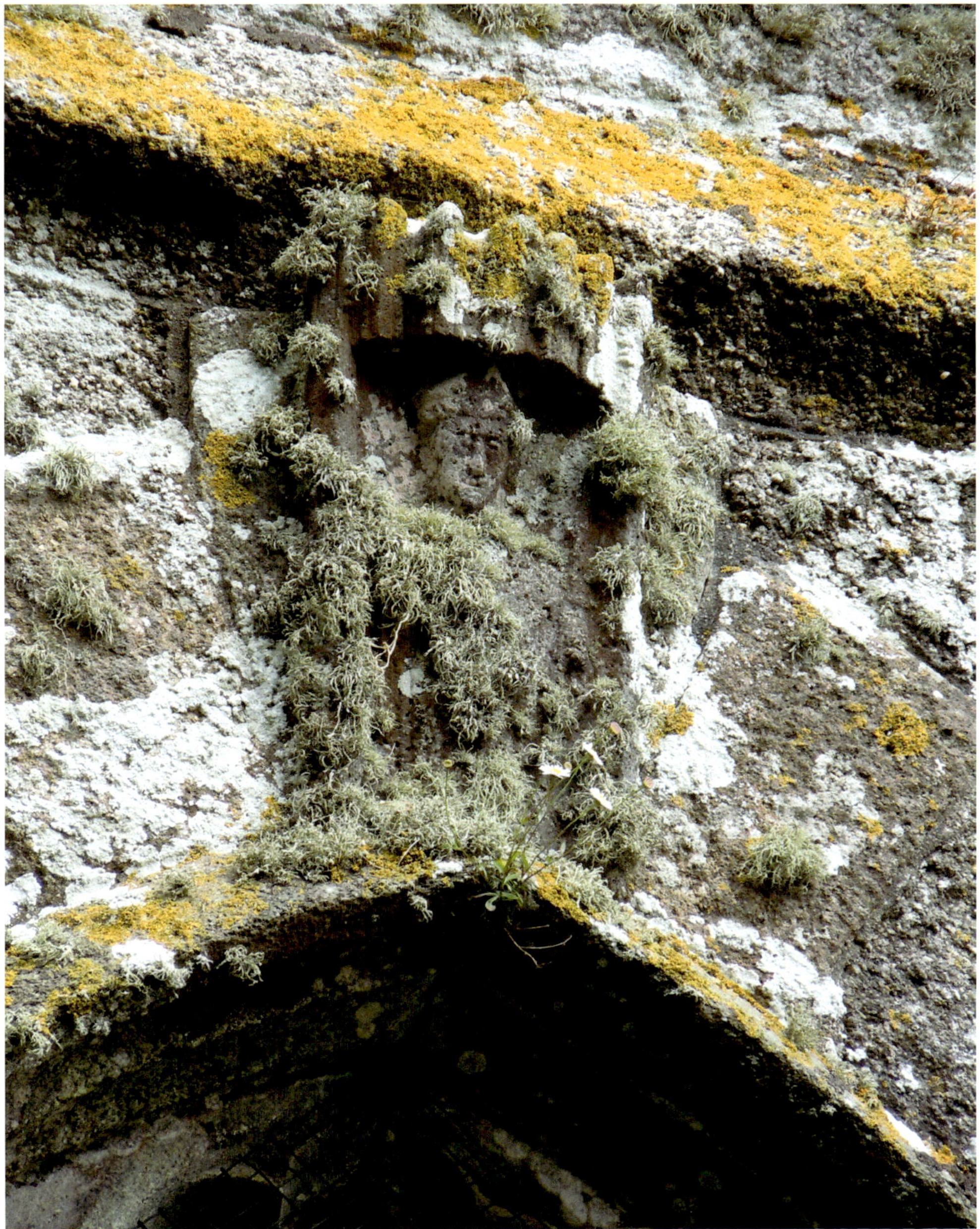

Mawgan in Meneage. Bishop over west window, fifteenth century.

A fifteenth-century tradition held that Maugan was bishop of the Isles of Scilly, but there was no such post. Bishops appear on side panels of Mawgan-in-Pydar lantern cross, with the smaller bishop there perhaps being the patronal saint.

Images of Christ, and occasionally the Holy Trinity, dominate west fronts of towers, just as they do lantern crosses. There are crucifixion panels on the west fronts of towers at Mullion and North Tamerton, a Risen Christ at St Austell with tiny donor figures, an almost obliterated Christ as St Saviour now inside Zennor church, and an IHC below the top niche at Paul. Part of a Christ figure remains on the west front of Combe Martin church tower in Devon. At 'St Mawe-in-the sand' – Mawgan-in-Pydar, not St Mawes – in 1537 there was a St Saviour image. This was on the outside of the north chancel wall of the parish church facing the street.

St Mary, the apostles and Evangelists were also common tower subjects. The Annunciation and apostles appear at St Austell, while at Paul a fleur-de-lys bracket

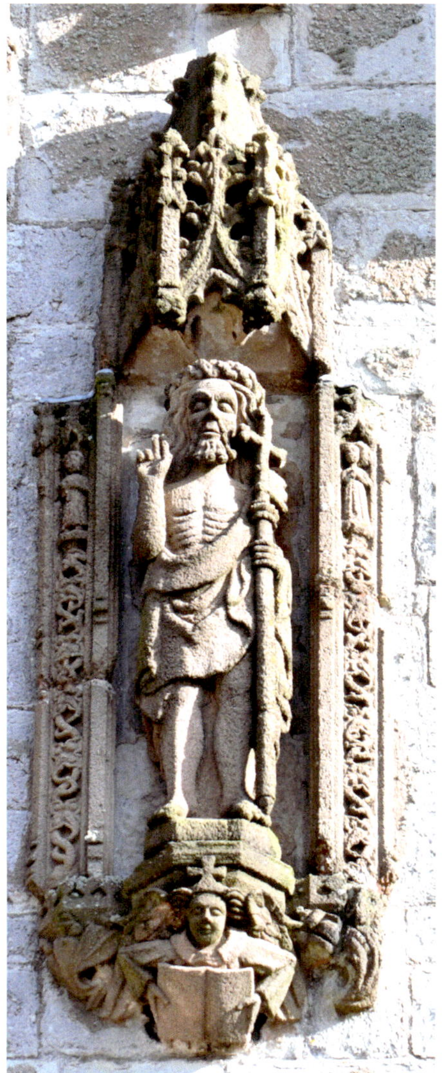

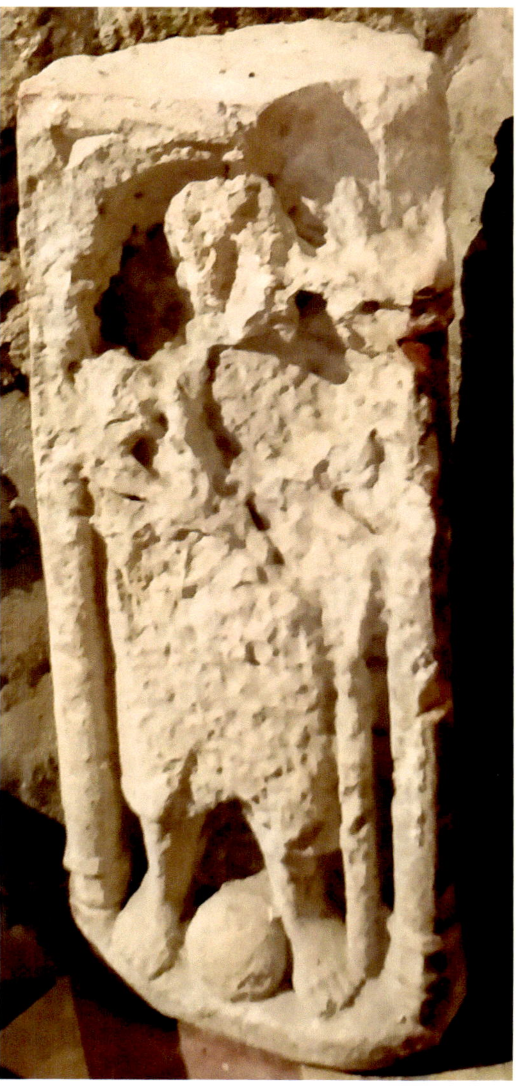

Above left: St Austell. Risen Christ, 1460s. (Photo by Ann Preston-Jones)

Above right: Zennor. Badly defaced Christ as Saviour of the World, fifteenth century.

to the left of the west window was for Mary as was the south niche at Week St Mary. Stockier early sixteenth-century apostles in short tunics appear just below the battlements of towers at St Dominick and South Hill. Evangelists or their symbols reside at different levels on the four corners of Callington, Gulval and St Mabyn towers. At Gulval, animal-headed Evangelists appear on a probable late eleventh-century cross base.

A probable St Sithney survives at battlement level by the south-east corner. Lanlivery's decorated tower corbels, low enough to be read from the ground, show lions flanking a wheat ear on the south-west, and angels with diadems implied wings carrying a female severed head on the south-east. Below the left angel is a large, bearded male head on its side, about twice the size of the female head, with lips parted and teeth showing. This looks like the slain giant Goliath in contemporary woodcut illustrations which medieval carvers used as models. A stylized sun that may be the Yorkist badge lies just below the right-hand angel.

It seems probable that these decorated corbels tell the otherwise lost story of Brivet, patron saint of Lanlivery, whose name in Latin is *Breve vita*, or short life. *Lives* of saints like Columb, Newlyn and Sidwell offer parallels and St Agnes had a giant tormentor, too. Like Endelient, Brivet had two wells, with the one nearer the church perhaps her place of martyrdom and Bribers Well her dwelling place. The wheat ear could signify that death took place at harvest time, as in the *Lives* of Devon saints Sidwell and Urith.

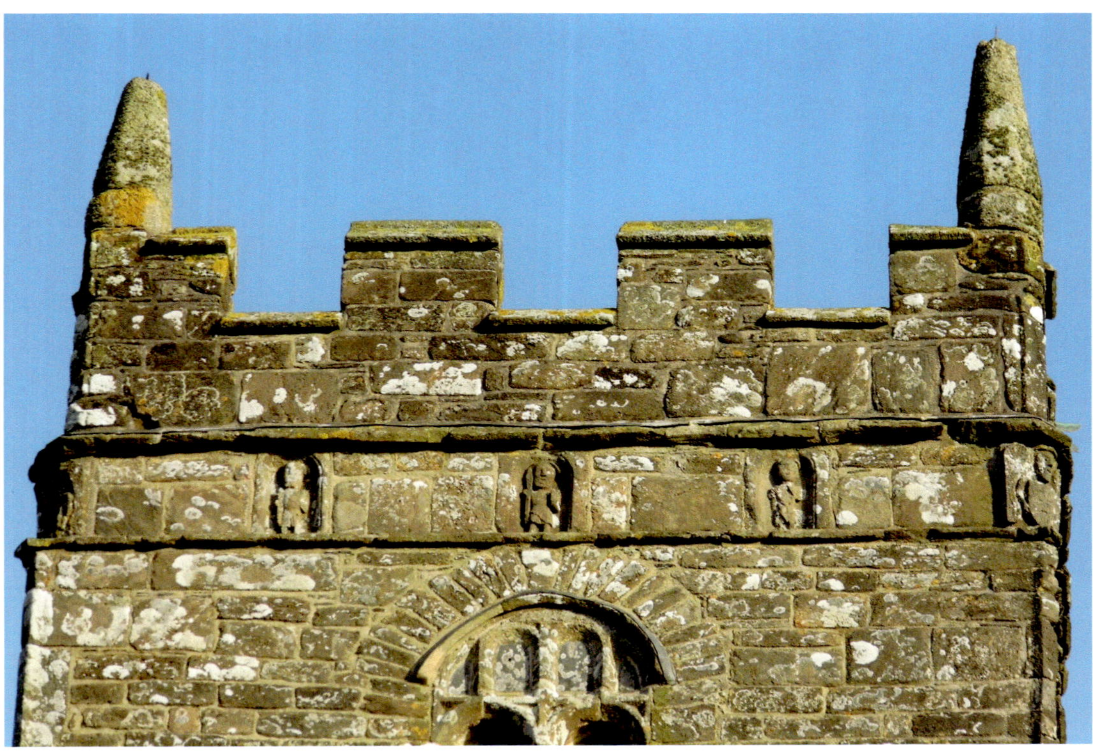

Southill. Tower apostles, early sixteenth century. (Photo by Andrew Langdon)

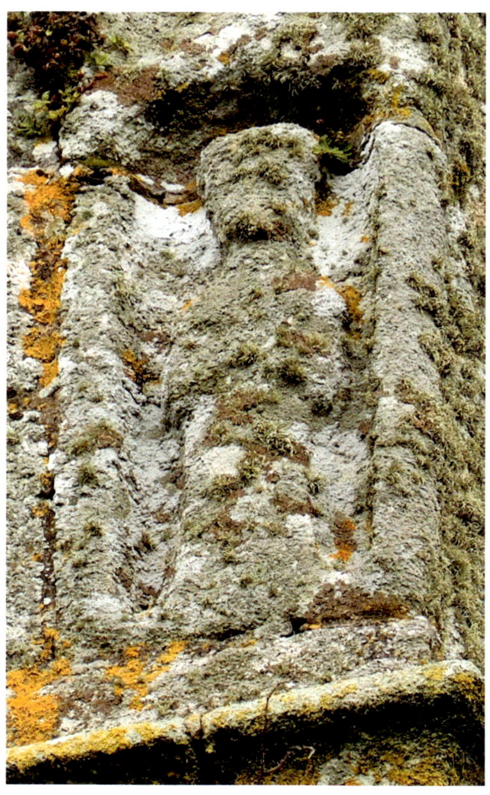

Right: Sithney. St Sithney, *c.* 1500.
(Photo by Nina Hocking)

Below: Lanlivery. Lions with wheat ear, 1460s.
(Photo by Pam Dodds)

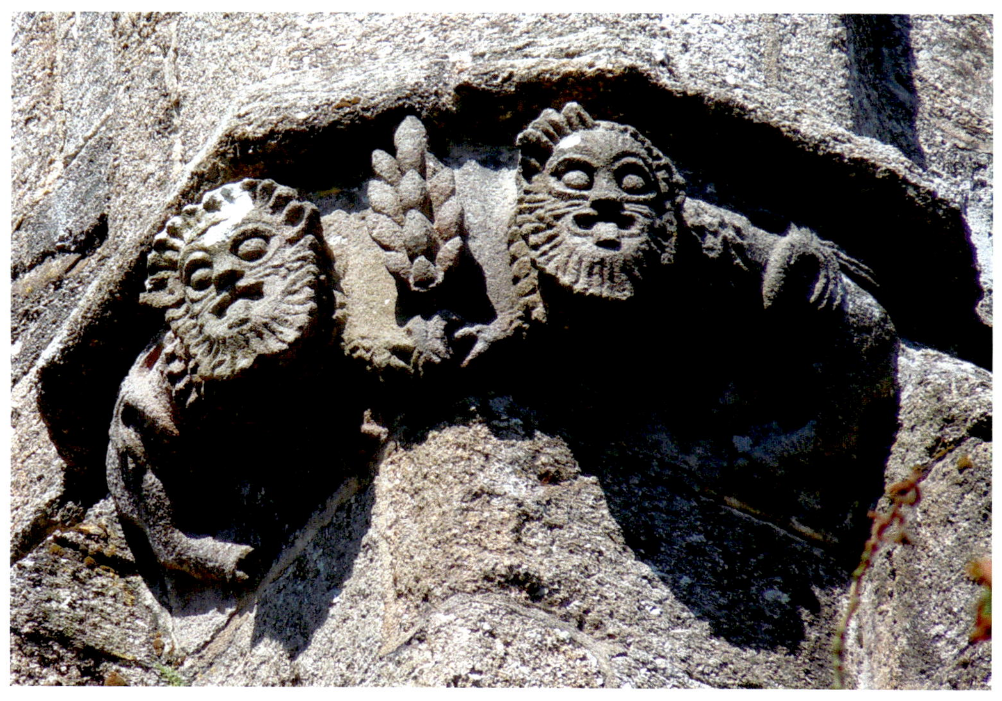

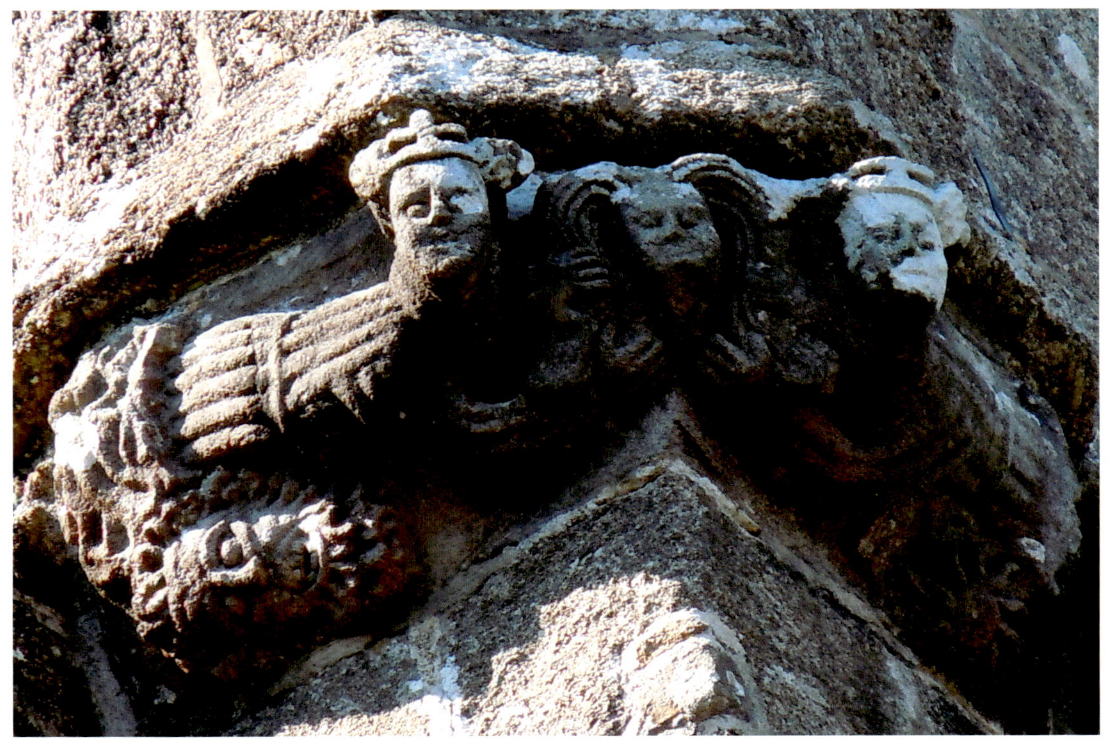

Lanlivery. Angels and severed heads, 1460s. (Photo by Pam Dodds)

The spire at Lostwithiel has tracery in the form of a wheel on its south side facing the bridge. This could represent St Katherine, probable dedicatee of a lost bridge chapel and patroness of the town's important medieval potteries. She appears on the churchyard lantern cross here and at Launceston. Heads on the hood moulds of tower and other doors are usually secular, but the base of the west door at Constantine has crowned heads that might allude to its patron saint. At Ladock there are distinctive corbels just above the roof on the east side of the tower; one at St Erme, now inside, shows a bearded male head probably intended for Erme or Hermes. It is unclear if the northern Ladock head is an angel with a hair robe or saint holding hair. This odd image could have given rise to the folk tale of Ladoc combing her hair too long while Probus brought his parish boundary ever closer.

Porches were places where marriage ceremonies took place and where baptism and churching of women after childbirth began, so an ideal location for Virgin and child images. Bodmin accounts mention a St Mary image in the porch but note that offerings ceased temporarily in 1469 during rebuilding. Porches with single external niches are common and include St Erth, Launceston St Mary Magdalene, Lelant and Luxulyan. Constantine church, which probably housed an important saint's tomb, had niches on both porches, and Bodmin and Liskeard have three southern niches suggestive of a Trinity and Annunciation like Plympton St Mary porch in Devon or St Austell tower. Although a possible Ludewan appears in low relief over the porch at Ludgvan today, he is not *in situ* (see p. 11).

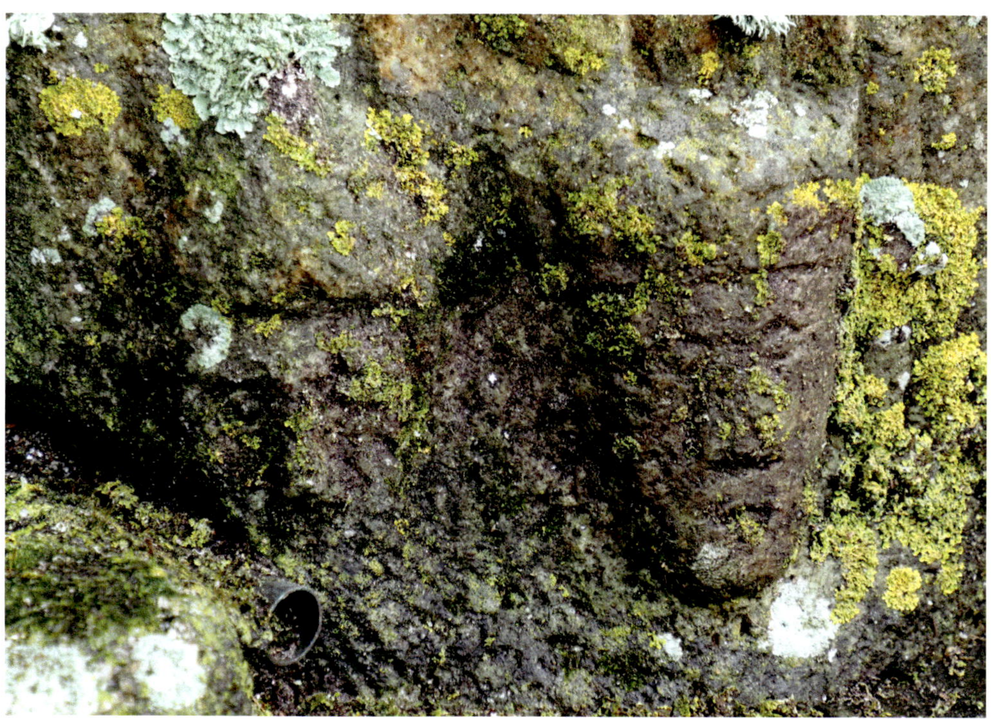

Above: Constantine. Crowned heads at west door base, fifteenth century. (Photo by Eric Berry)

Right: St Erme: Erme or Hermes corbel head, *c.* 1500. (Photo by Nina Hocking)

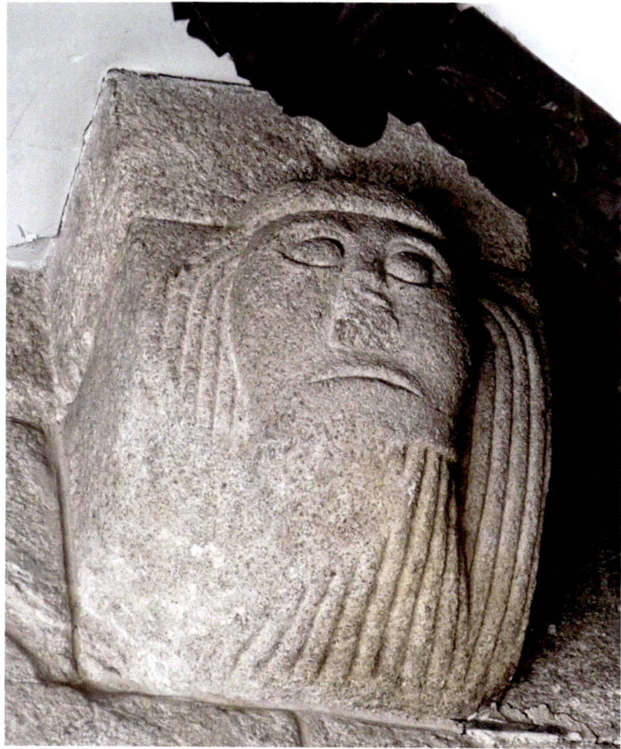

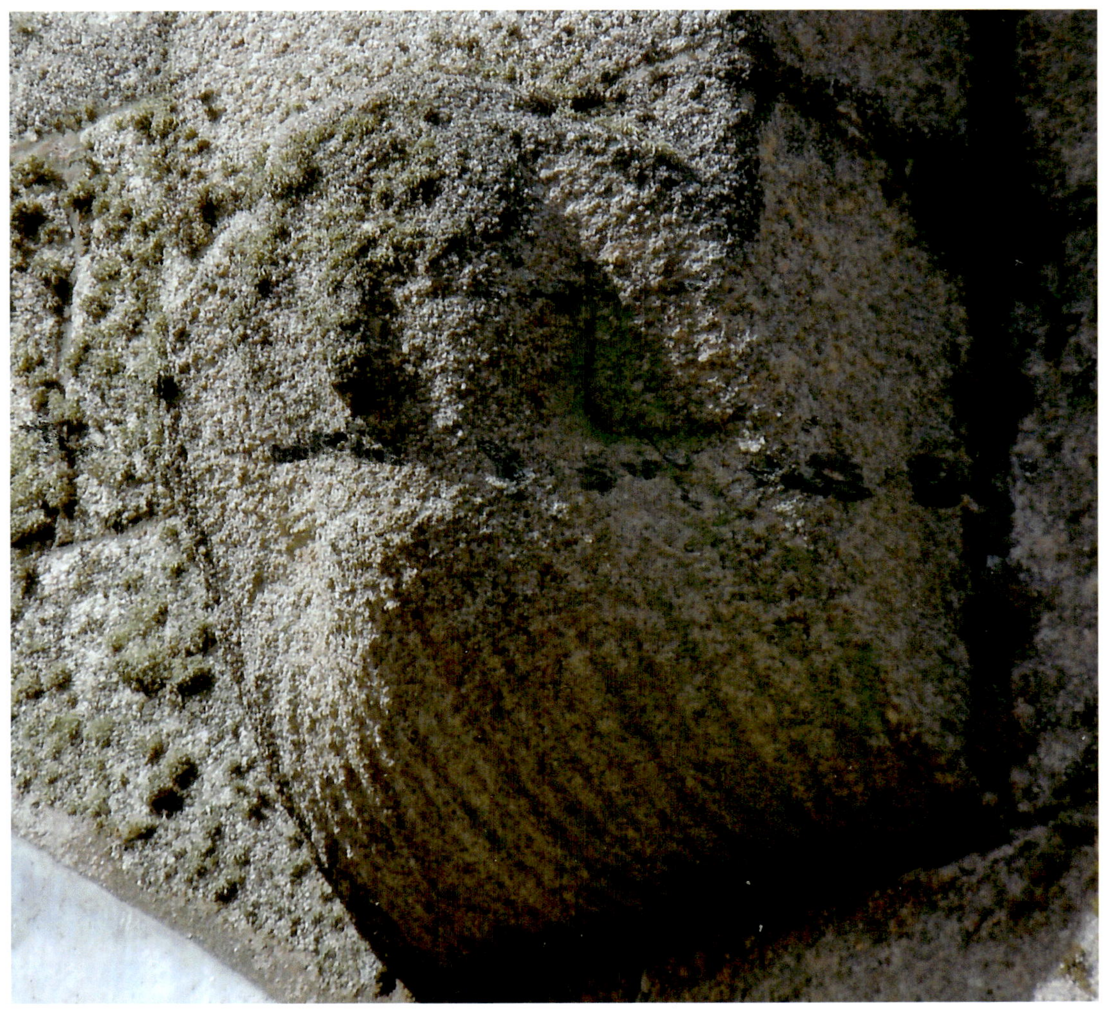

Ladock. tower corbel, *c.* 1500. (Photos by Geoffrey Holborough)

Image niches and corbels are more common inside porches, where candles could be burnt before a statue. Good single examples include Budock, St Endellion, Fowey and St Newlyn East. A squat bishop over the south door at St Keverne may depict the local saint, being previously loose in the church with reliquary and shrine fragments. At Landulph a headless saint in the niche is likely to be Mary not Dilic or Leonard. The internal porch niche at Poughill has a bracket on the left, perhaps for Olaf, with flanking brackets at Lanreath suggesting joint patrons Manac and Dunstan as well as Mary. At Mabe a bracket directly below the niche once held a candle.

Launceston St Mary Magdalene's 1511 porch exterior is the most highly decorated of any Cornish porch. The central niche has horizontal panels carved in low relief on each side: St George to the left killing the dragon and St Martin to the right. Martin, wearing a Tudor flat cap, is shown on horseback cutting his cloak in half with his sword to share

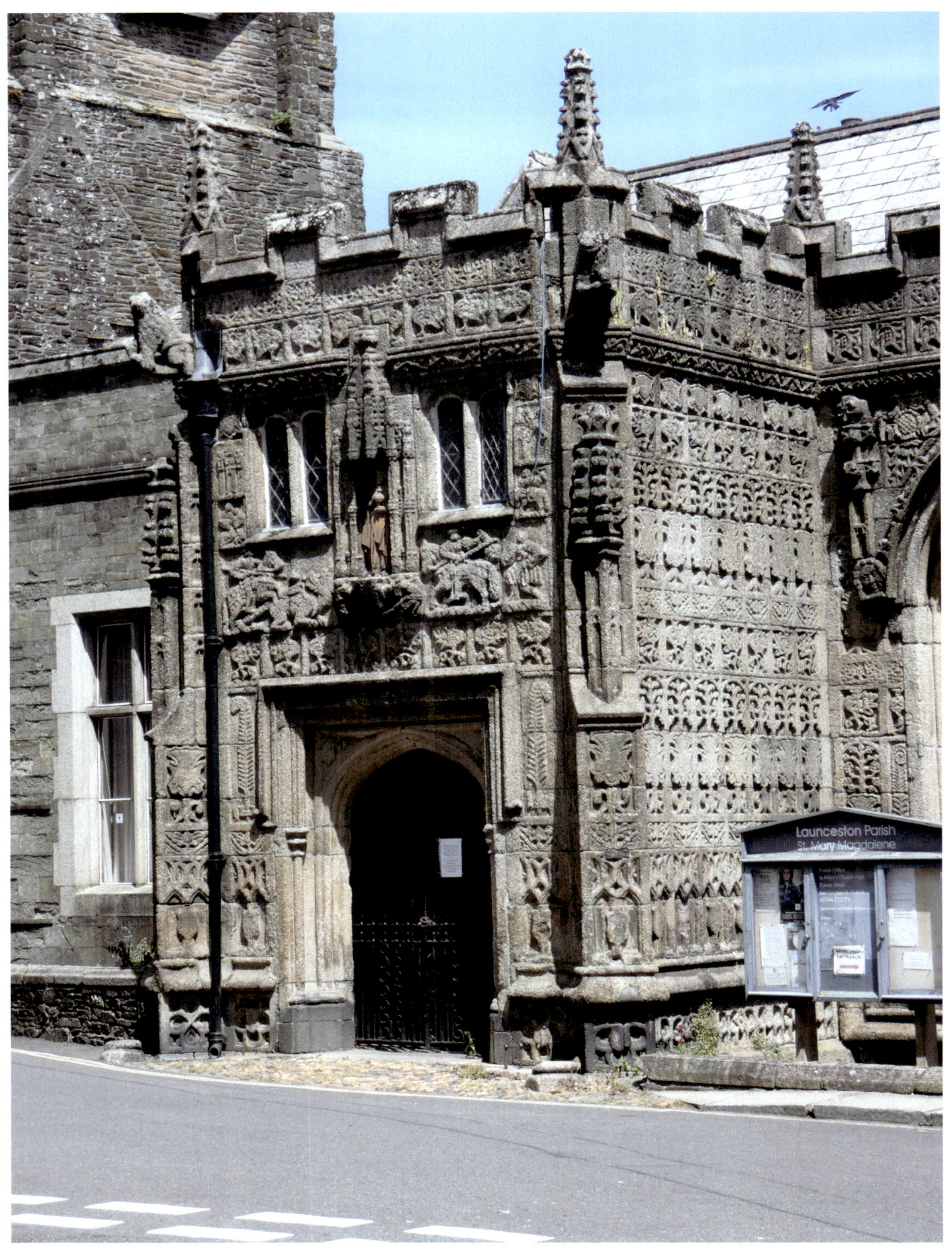

Launceston St Mary Magdalene. Porch, 1511. (Photo by Ann Preston-Jones)

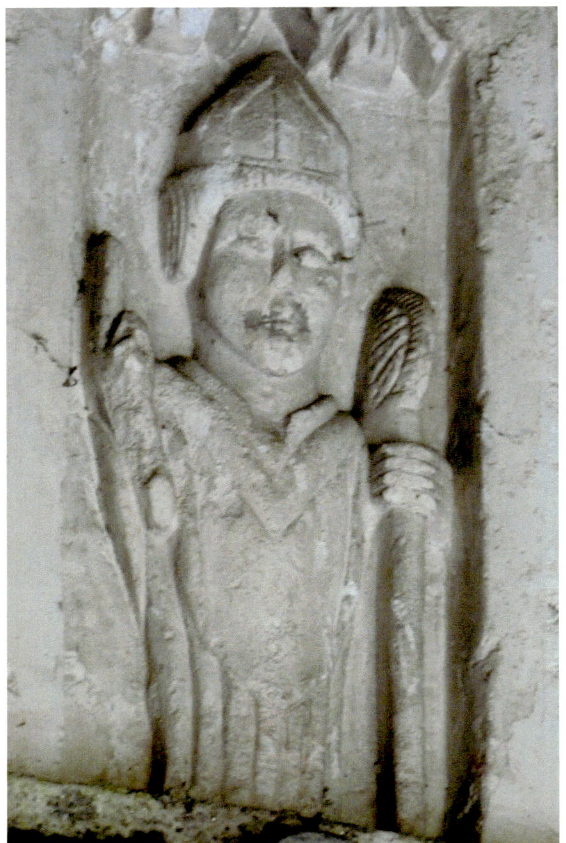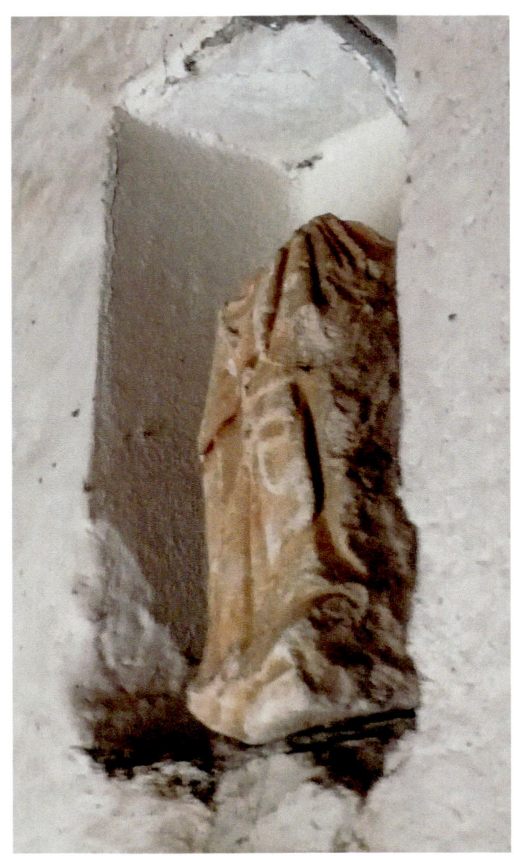

Above left: St Keverne. Bishop, medieval. (Photo by Andrew Langdon)

Above right: Landulph. Headless saint, medieval.

with a beggar who genuflects thanks. The worn panel above St George could be a Virgin and Child, while there is a windmill over Martin; Martin being patron of mill workers at Bodmin. A gable trefoil-lobed cross on Germoe porch shows the crucified Christ, with Reynard the Fox moralistic imagery lower down. On the exterior of porches at St Austell and St Enoder the pious pelican, who in mythology pecked her breast to feed blood to her young, stands in for Christ and his five wounds.

Modern copies of shields of Christ's Passion adorn south aisle buttresses at St Austell, while sacred monograms – a stylized G for Jesus and M for Mary – can be found on label stops of St Just-in-Penwith's south aisle windows. The former south aisle of St Mary's parish church, now part of Truro Cathedral, still has over thirty external niches, the largest number of any church in Cornwall.

At Truro St Mary and Launceston St Mary Magdalene the Tudor royal coat of arms appears on the east gable as St Columb and a dove may have done once at St Columb Major. Below the east window at Launceston there is a large niched figure of St Mary Magdalene veiled and barefoot. As the arch-sinner of the New Testament, she is shown

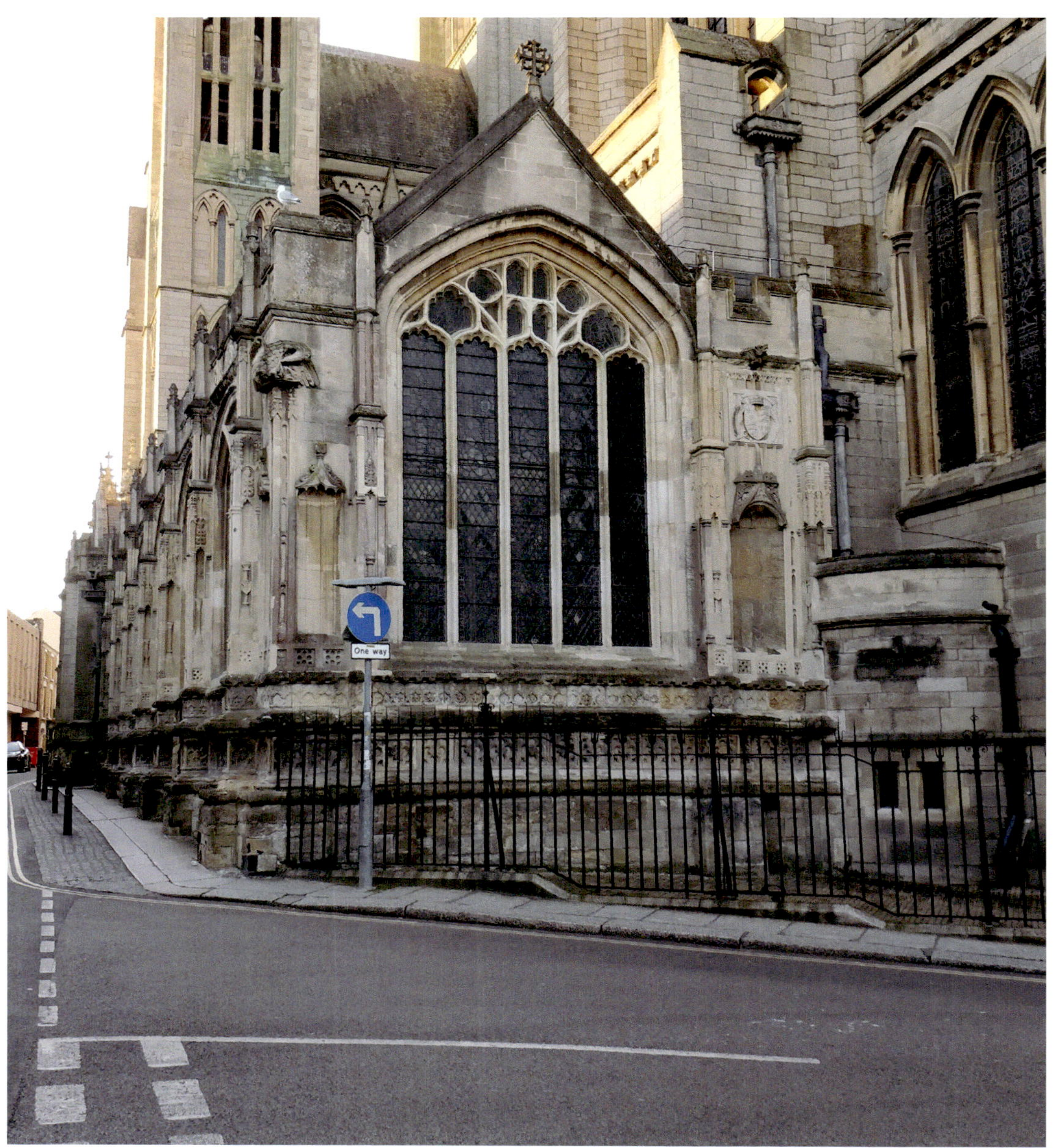

Truro Cathedral. St Mary's aisle, 1504–18.

'creeping to the cross', a repentance ceremony performed inside the church on Good Friday. With an ointment pot used for anointing feet by her side, carved minstrels celebrate her repentance. How this splendid east-end sculpture survived the iconoclasts or image breakers is unclear, but perhaps she was plastered over. Mary Magdalene also appears twice on a nearby lantern cross. Panels showing an eleventh-century Christ in Majesty and a Virgin and Child now displayed on the east wall of the chancel of St Stephen-by-Launceston church were probably originally internal sculptures.

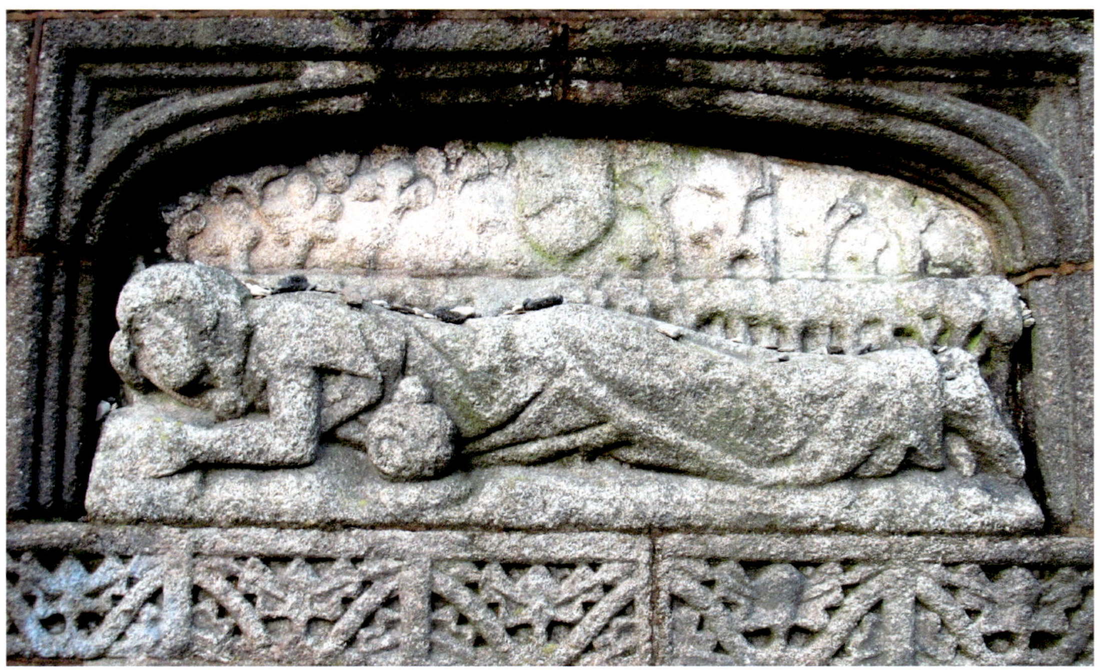

Launceston St Mary Magdalene. Mary Magdalene, 1520s. (Photo by Ann Preston-Jones)

The focus on Christ and Mary among Cornwall's seventeen late medieval lantern crosses, named for their resemblance to medieval lanterns and with a small cross on top, echoes the tower and porch hierarchies discussed above. These late medieval church and chapel-yard crosses are found all over England and Wales, but only Somerset has more examples than Cornwall. Patron saints, whether international like Bartholomew at Lostwithiel or local like Maugan at Mawgan-in-Pydar or Newlyn at St Newlyn East, were relegated to side panels. The front of these once splendid sculptural creations was reserved for Christ crucified or occasionally a Trinity image, and the back for Mary. Usually seated with a crown, child or sceptre, at Mawgan-in-Pydar there is an Annunciation scene and at Launceston she is accompanied by St Mary Magdalene and St Katherine. A panel of carving in the guildhouse wall opposite Tywardreath church, probably from the priory, may depict Tobias and the angel. Iconoclasm and weathering mean few local lantern cross saints are now recognisable, and it is even unclear if Newlyn, depicted with spare head in hands, originally had two heads.

Stone Saints Within

Starting in the chancel at St Issey, a probable daughter of Brychan, we find a remarkable tomb shrine, now a reredos. Of 1390s–1430s date, Issey's shrine may have doubled as the tomb of Lady Matilda Chyverston: an indulgence of 1399 gave visitors to her tomb at St Issey time off from purgatory. The shrine top, where any indulgence inscription and heraldry might have been, is long lost. First noted in 1753 when in use as the tower step, the frieze of worn figures was described as armed knights and their wives. Nikolaus

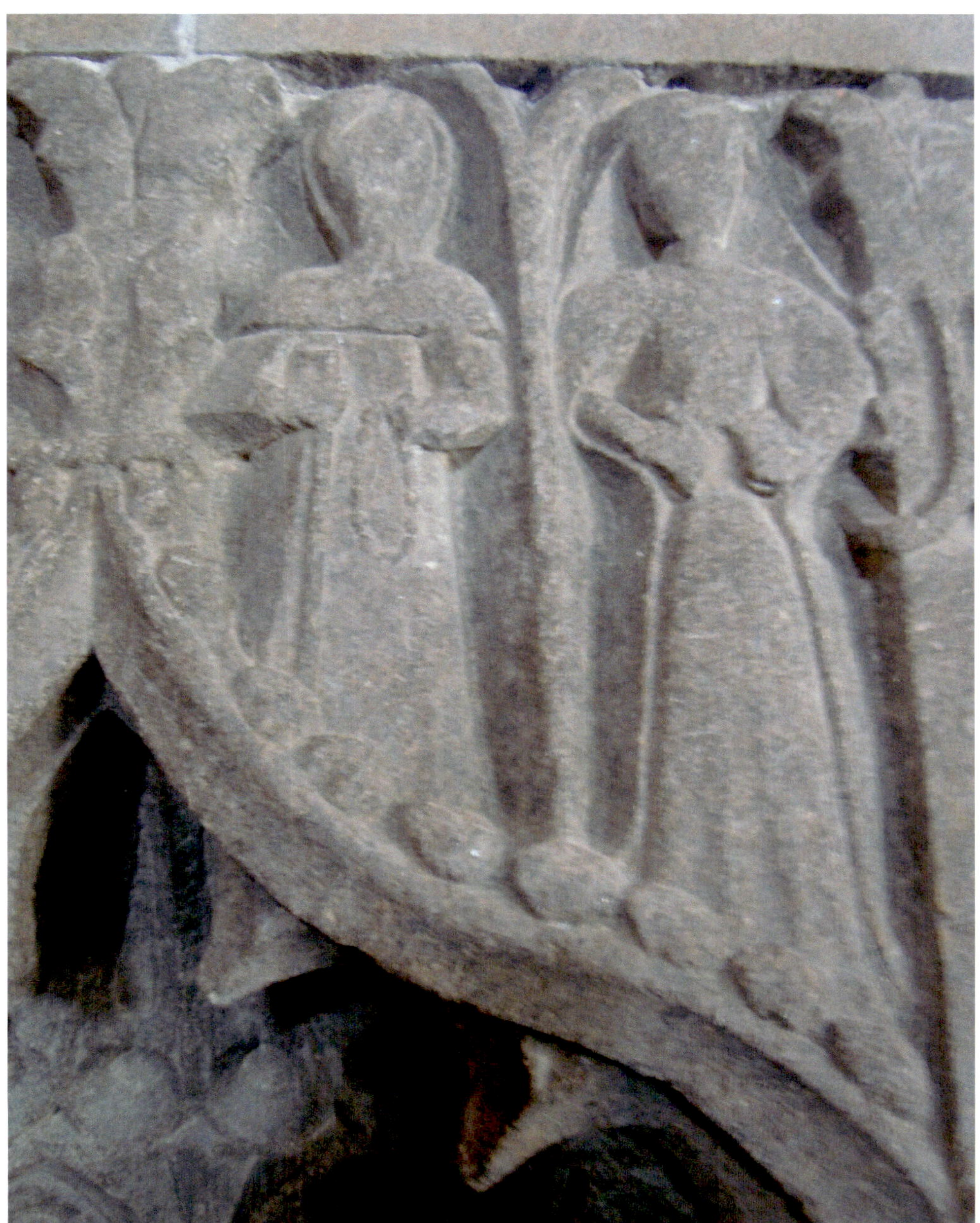

St Issey. Shrine, first panel detail, 1390s–1430s.

Pevsner in 1951 saw little angels through his pebble glasses, and more recently Peter Beacham suggested ecclesiastics and laymen.

In fact, there are twelve male and eight female saints lacking facial features due to the passage of feet. The men have very short haircuts and vestment-style gowns, the women pleated gowns with simple veils. These seem to be twenty of the twenty-four Children

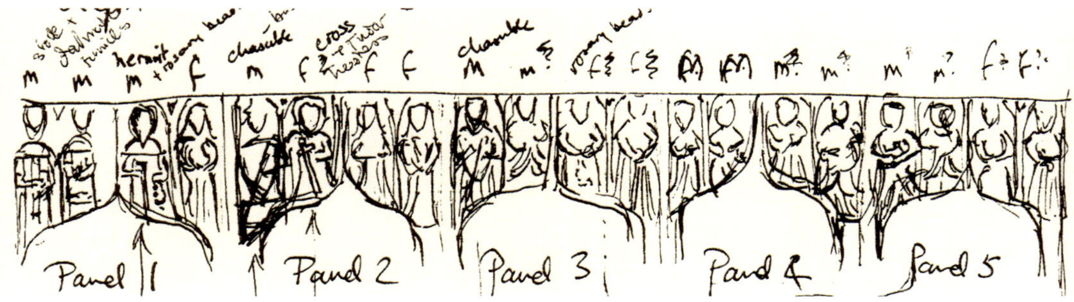

St Issey. Rough sketch used to work out gender.

of Brychan and they appear in groups of four over five niches. Ironically, Issey is not shown as the front panel is missing. On the remaining side, the first three figures are male. One holds a cross and could be Nectan of Hartland, the second a bottle or flask, while the third has a hood, staff and rosary beads, the last figure being a wimpled female. The fifth and sixth figures are a mitred bishop and abbess, followed by two more women. The ninth and tenth figures are both male, the first holding a short staff and wearing a chasuble. They are followed by two females, the first holding rosary beads. A panel of four men comes next, and the final panel shows two men and two women. This gender patterning suggests that a panel of four women is missing from the start of the sequence. The Children of Brychan were also celebrated by a song or hymn sung *c.* 1500 in Mabyn's honour at St Mabyn.

Alabaster reredoses were desirable, colourful and affordable imports into Cornwall from the Midlands, but some at St Michael's Mount, Falmouth and Treslothan may be post-Reformation imports. As early as 1337, there was an alabaster image of Mary the Virgin in Restormel chapel, Lostwithiel and today alabaster fragments survive in at least ten Cornish churches and one chapel. These include the top part of a St Christopher at St Ive and the nine orders of angels at Madron. Finds made in the nineteenth century but now lost at Cury and Sennen included Christ and the apostles.

The most complete medieval alabaster reredos in Cornwall is now in pieces at Mabe. Two panels come from a *Life* of the Virgin Mary, including the announcement to Joachim with Joachim and Anne's meeting at the Golden Gate, and the Dedication of the Virgin in the Temple. These were matched by two scenes from the *Life* of Christ showing the Presentation in the Temple and Flagellation. There is also a St John the Evangelist being boiled alive in a cauldron (see p. 87), and a headless St Stephen holding stones. Torture scenes were popular reredos subjects and include Bartholomew flayed at Lostwithiel, Lawrence grilled on a gridiron at Lanteglos-by-Fowey and the lower part of Peter chained at St Cleer. There are nine orders of angels at Madron, a headless Trinity at Sithney, the Last Judgement and Christ stepping out of his tomb at Lanlivery, a possible seated Virgin at Crantock and an unidentified male saint's head in the chapel at Camelford.

A local saint, Petroc, makes two appearances in Catacleuse carvings at St Issey and over the chancel piscina at Padstow. At St Issey, Petroc was part of the original chancel reredos, now in the Lady Chapel. Dressed as a hermit with staff and bell, he is paired with

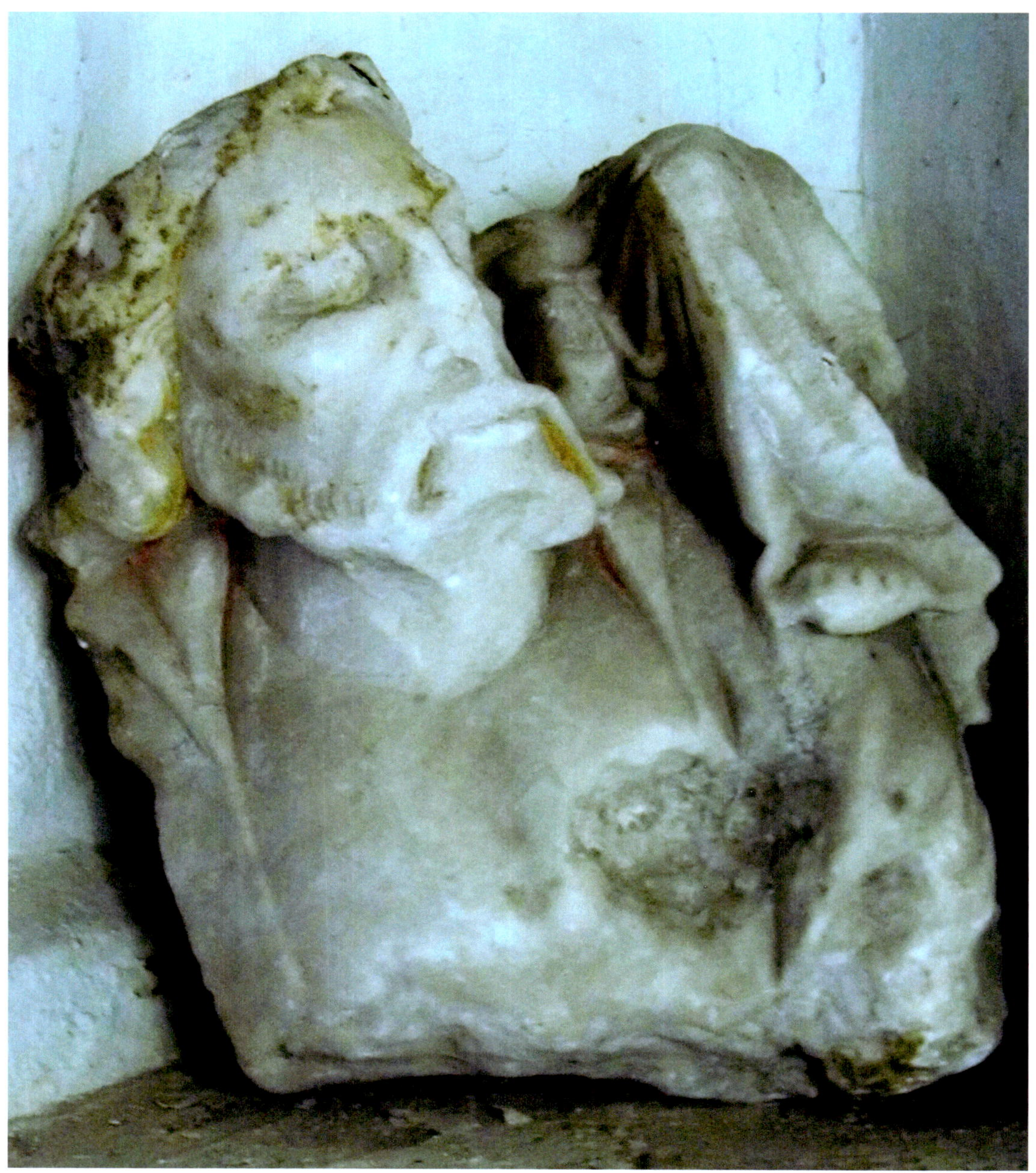

St Ive. St Christopher, alabaster, fourteenth century. (Photo by Andrew Langdon)

a possible Nectan over a pietà. Both Petroc images show the deer saved from Constantine, who had a chapel in St Merryn parish nearby.

At Kenwyn, a bishop on the south capital of the north transept arch surely represents Kenwyn, while Dennis appears on the north side of the tower arch at St Dennis missing his right hand and second head. A possible Trinity sequence occurs in the Lady Chapel

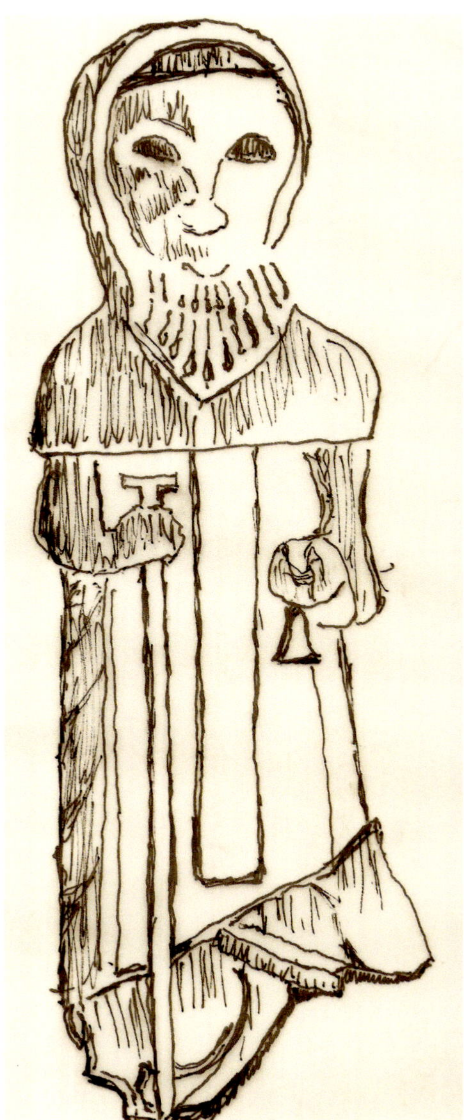

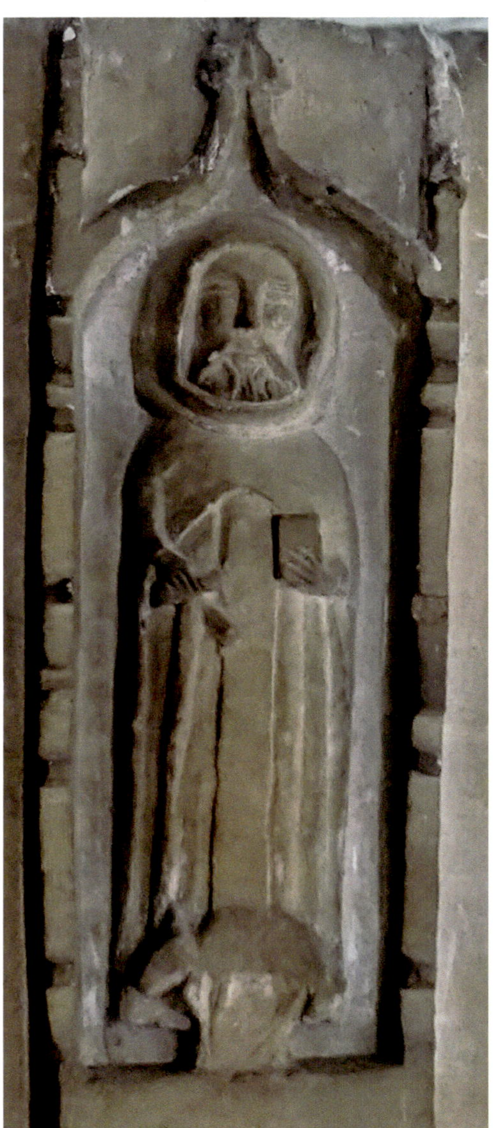

Above left: St Issey. Drawing of St Petroc with staff, bell and deer, Lady Chapel reredos detail, 1390s–1430s.

Above right: Padstow. St Petroc and deer, piscina, fifteenth century.

window splay at St Gluvias. Capitals at St Just in Penwith have sacred monograms, and at St Mabyn INRI references the rood (see *Churches of Cornwall*, p. 57).

Three-dimensional statues were vulnerable to attack by image breakers, especially inside churches where they were foci of devotion or cults, but no local saint has been found so far. A life-size head of Mary at St Allen, a large seated Mary without head at Talland and a headless Mary at Sennen restored with child in clay survive, with two parts

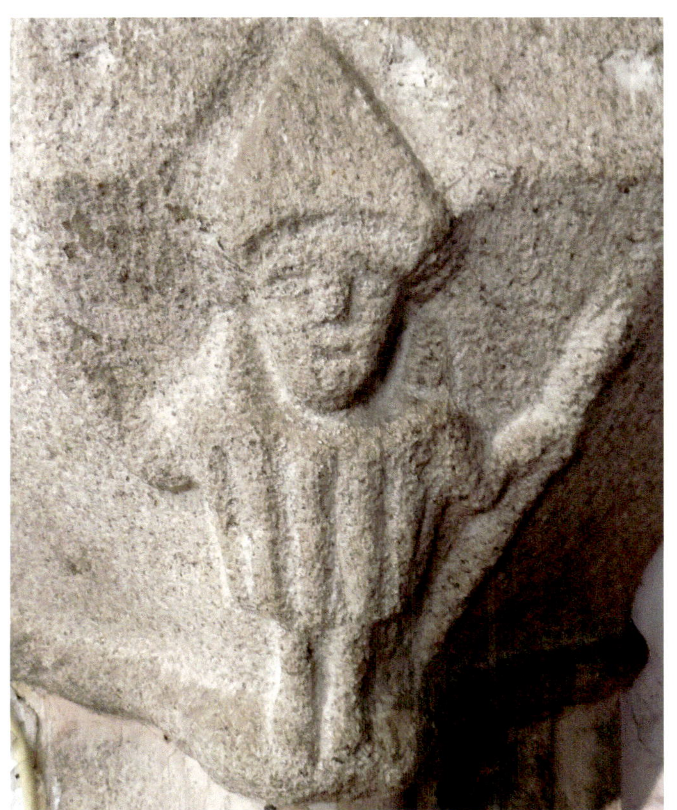

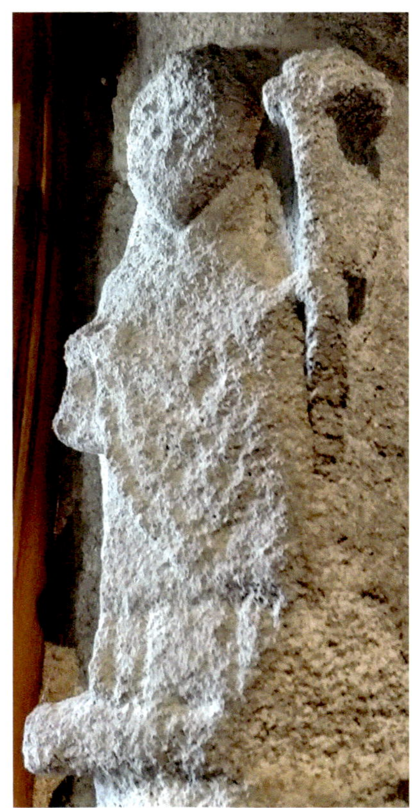

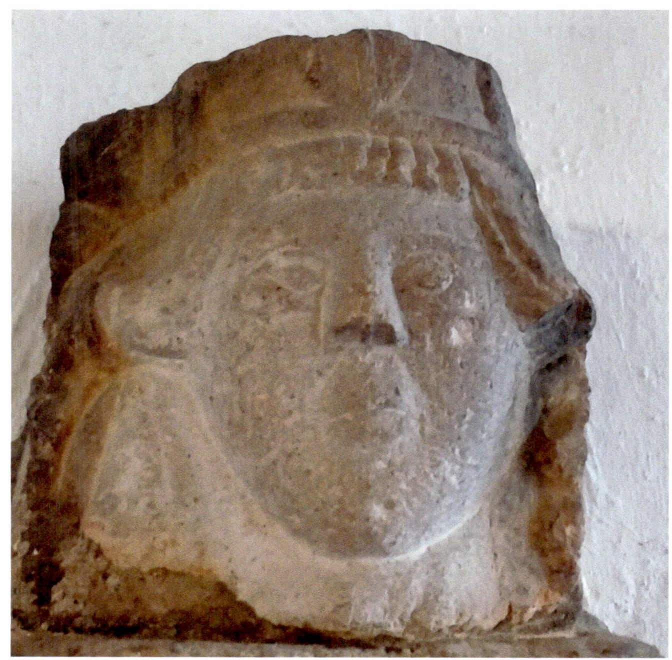

Above left: Kenwyn. Bishop, fifteenth century.

Above right: St Dennis. Bishop, late fifteenth century.

Right: St Allen. Life-size head of St Mary, early sixteenth century.

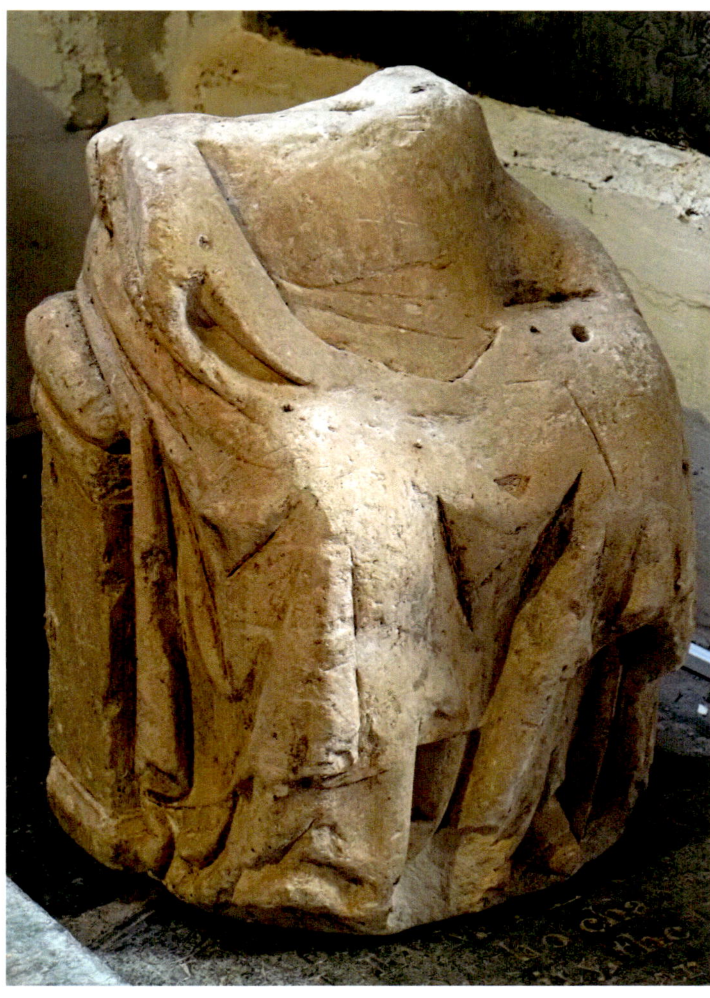

Talland. Headless seated St Mary, medieval. (Photo by Eric Berry)

of a headless limestone statue of St John Baptist at St Kew, with camel head by the saint's foot represent quality carving.

Statues of James can be seen at the Old School in St Breward and Perranuthnoe church and St Antony from Merther at Tresillian (see p. 21). A St Stephen statue was found in 1849 hidden at Browda in Linkinhorne but then lost, while a limestone corbel in Mawnan church depicts a bishop.

Fifteenth-century Catacleuse fonts show twelve apostles at St Merryn (formerly at Constantine chapel) and Padstow. Other font carvings include a fourteenth-century crucifixion at Lostwithiel, and a Virgin and Child and three Christs, but no St Piran, at Perranzabuloe. Withiel has an early fifteenth-century font with three anchors for their patron saint Clement and the saint combined with a fourth anchor to represent his means of martyrdom. Saints appeared on tombs with a defaced Crucifixion on the end of the 1485 tomb of Sir John Colshull at Duloe and four Renaissance Evangelists writing gospels on the base of Prior Vivian's 1534 Catacleuse tomb at Bodmin.

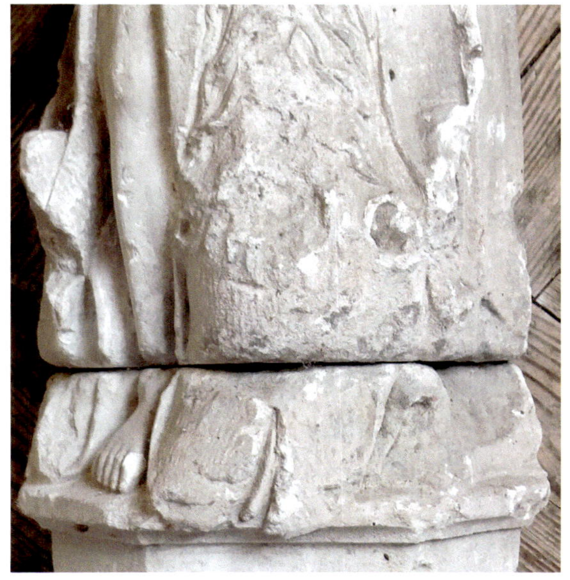

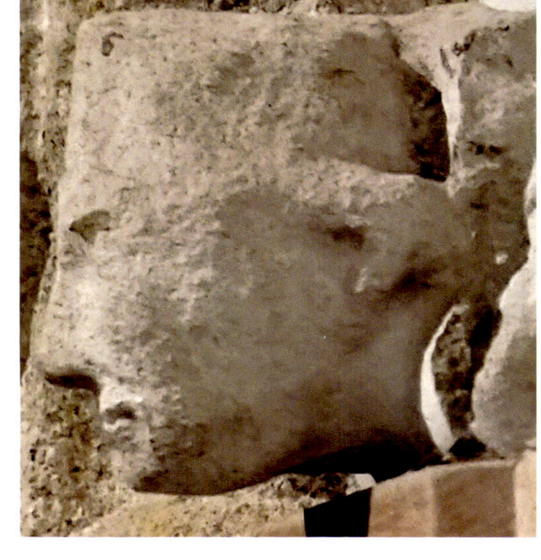

Above left: St Kew. St John Baptist's camel head with open mouth and tongue, fifteenth century.

Above right: Mawnan. Bishop corbel, fourteenth century.

Right: Withiel. St Clement anchorman, font stem, early fifteenth century.

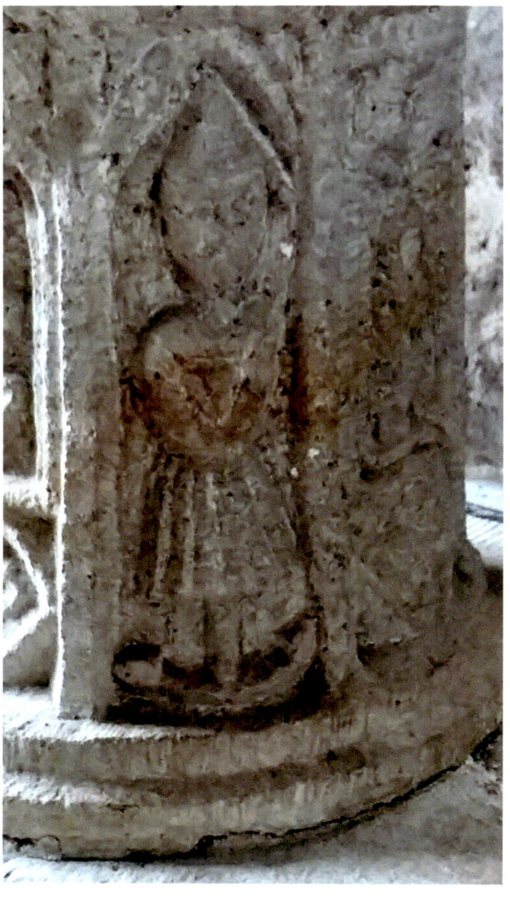

4. Saints of Wood, Metal and Thread

St Sampson Golant, a former chapelry of Tywardreath, has an early sixteenth-century south aisle, chancel and nave. Set in a wildlife churchyard above the river Fowey, the church still contains one of the best collections of saint-related Cornish woodwork, notably roof inscriptions, a probable rood loft figure and recycled bench-ends.

Inscriptions carved in low relief around the nave wall plates are hard to read now but fortunately were transcribed. Reading from east to west on the south side and west to east on the north nave, inscriptions name six parish guilds of All Saints, Eloy, George, James, John and Katherine, with a seventh guild of Samson implied.

Guilds were the medieval equivalent of friendly societies or burial clubs. Usually comprising twelve to twenty-four male and female members, they met once a year to settle accounts, attend Mass and feast together. At least 165 guilds are documented in Cornwall, including unspecified guilds in six parishes. Thirty-four guilds were in Bodmin parish, including five trade guilds, but rural parishes like Antony, Camborne and North Petherwin had ten or eleven each. At Camborne, six of the eleven guilds were associated with chapels in the parish.

Only sixteen local and Brittonic guild saints are recorded, due to a dearth of West Cornwall churchwardens' accounts apart from Camborne, such accounts providing the best evidence for multiple guilds. Brittonic guild saints included Grade and Gwinear, Lallu at Menheniot, Meriadec at Camborne, Patern at North Petherwin, Petroc at Bodmin, Piran at Perranuthnoe and chapel guilds of Anta at Lelant, David at Bodmin, Derwa, Ia and Winwalloe at Camborne, Kew at St Kew (churchyard chapel) and Werys at St Breock. There were also stores of Cadoc at Padstow and Naunter at Creed, these being looser associations providing wax or renting out animals.

At St Sampson Golant a small panel, probably depicting St Samson, is now part of the pulpit. This may have come from the loft that once topped the lost chancel screen, known together as the rood loft. Samson's shoulder-length hairstyle resembles images in Anglo-Saxon gospel books. Although bearded, Samson has no moustache, like many early sixteenth-century Cornish saints' images. He wears a long gown buttoned at the top with a cloak thrown over it, his feet are bare and he holds a cross with a key-like handle in his right hand and a book in his left. This carving, like the bench-ends in Golant church, includes a backstaff, an early navigational aid and badge of the local Colquite family.

Samson's *Life* is the earliest to survive in Cornwall and was written at Dol in Brittany in the eighth century, two hundred years after the saint's death. The anonymous author calls Samson 'Confessor of Jesus Christ'. He was said to be of noble birth, schooled at Llantwit

Major, Wales, where he became a priest and moved to Caldey island. Samson converted his father and the rest of his family before slaying his first serpent, visiting Ireland and becoming a hermit and abbot.

The next seven chapters are set in Cornwall: Samson was unwelcome at Docco monastery in St Kew parish, where the rules had grown lax, so travelled around Cornwall in a two-horse chariot with holy vessels and books. Encountering pagans worshipping an abominable image, he 'defused' this by carving a cross on it. Samson then cured a young boy who had broken his neck falling from a horse at the pagan games, but had to kill a second cave-dwelling serpent to achieve mass conversion. A thirst-quenching holy well was created in the serpent's cave and Samson's father became head of a new monastery probably at South Hill. Samson left Cornwall to become bishop of Dol.

There are other wooden figure panels, not all religious, of varying sizes that might have come from the galleried-fronts of Cornish rood lofts. As well as apostles – Andrew at St Ives, Bartholomew at Braddock, James the Great at St Levan, Peter at Braddock and St Ives – there are similar figures of Christ, depicted as a shepherd with a sheep at Tregaminion chapel, reputedly from Tywardreath church and as St Saviour at Tywardreath. Other possible loft statues include the intercessor St John the Baptist

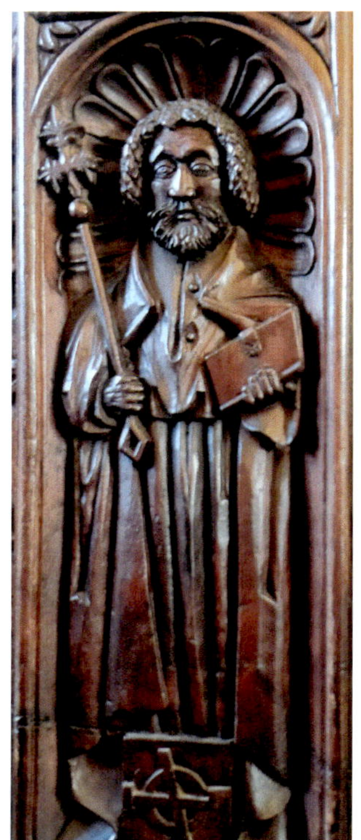
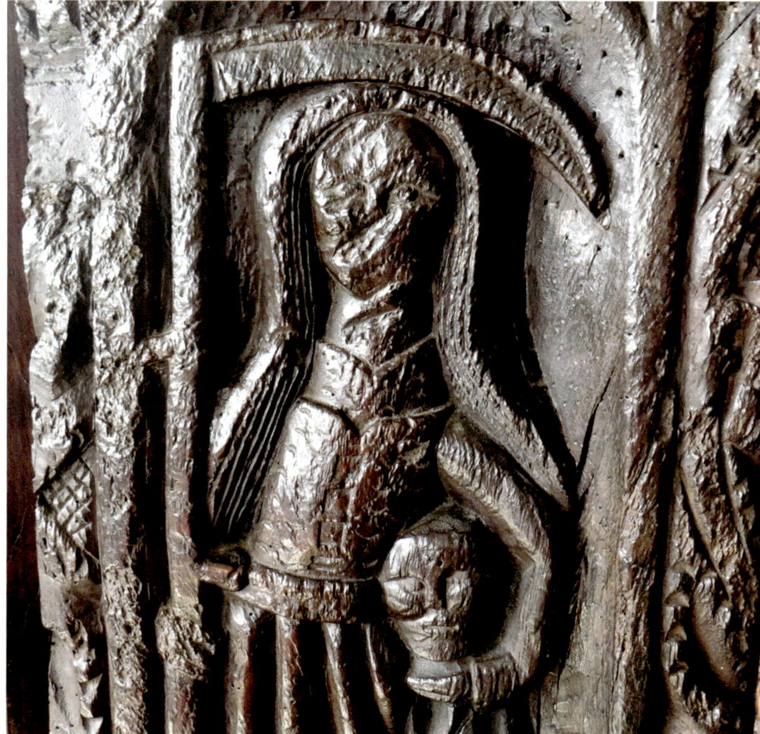

Above left: St Sampson Golant. St Samson panel, early sixteenth century.

Above right: Braddock. St Sidwell detail, early sixteenth century.

at Antony (where four Evangelist panels form part of the pulpit), and a scythe-wielding, veil-wearing Sidwell carrying an extra head under her arm at Braddock. Two fools at St Levan complete these survivals, though pairs of sibyls at Cardinham and Mullion could have come from loft or dado. Cardinham also has two coronations of the virgin panels, now part of a chest.

Roofs are dark and desolate places rather than the glorious painted and angel-populated Catholic heaven. Many chancel roofs date from Victorian restorations. Saints, if they appear at all, had to share this space with heraldry and secular faces – young men (Poughill), a gurning man (St Neot) and green men (St Eval and Lanlivery). Relgious symbols on roof bosses include three nails at Egloshayle, a pious pelican at Morwenstow, and a Trinity of three hares sharing ears at Cotehele.

Local saints' symbols appear at St Neot in a wooden retelling of the story of his three fish (see *Churches of Cornwall* p. 69). Told in shorthand form on four roof bosses, the full version appears in the stained-glass window of his *Life* further west (n7, see p. 64). On the bosses, fish poke their heads out of swirling water, first three, then only one emerging further in alarm as the instruction to take one fish a day is disobeyed, then a half floral boss, a fish on a gridiron, and finally two fish served up on leaves. A triangle of Neot's fish appears on Crowland Abbey screen dado in Lincolnshire with St Guthlac, and more

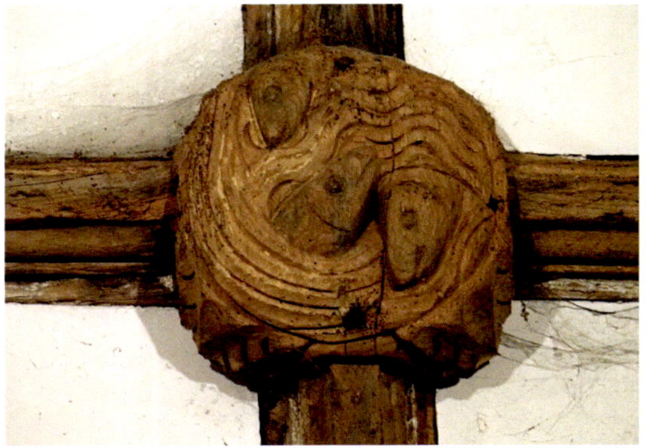
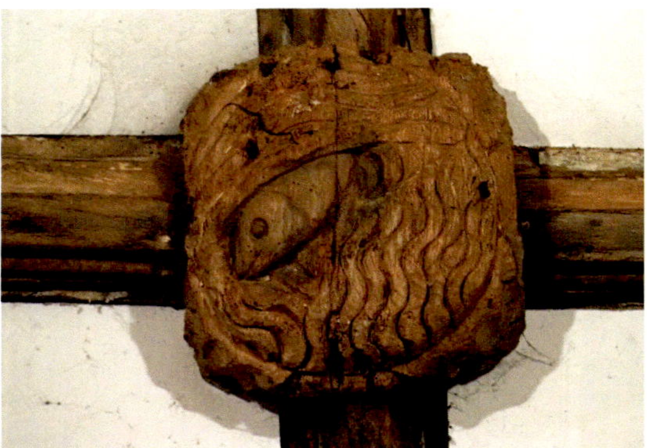
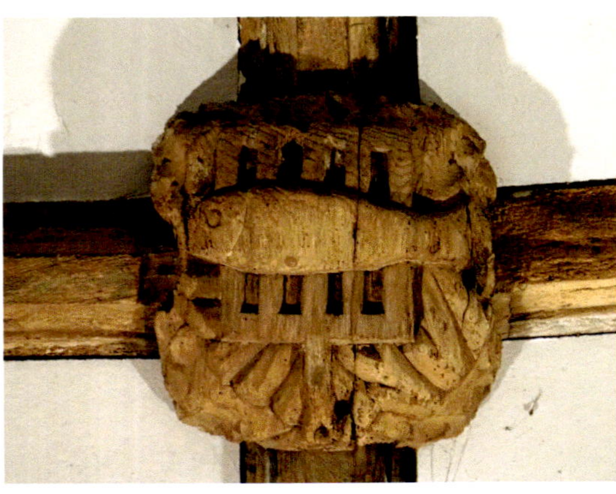
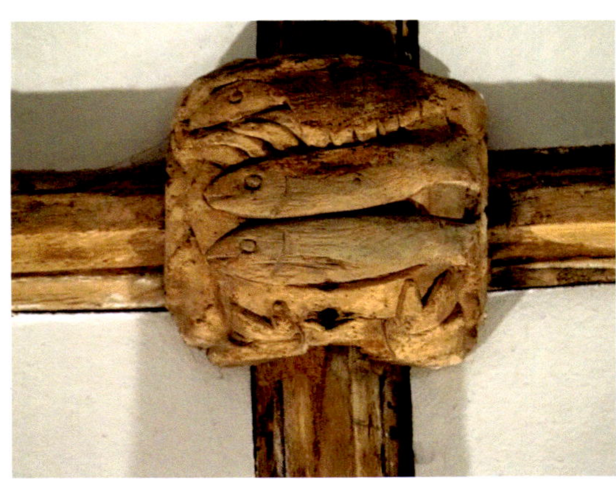

St Neot. Four roof bosses showing story of Neot's fish, 1530s. (Photos by Eric Berry)

fish swim in the south aisle roof of St Neots, Huntingdonshire, around the old entrance. At Laneast a crowned female head roof boss in the chancel may well be Sidwell, Saxon patroness of the church and a major Devon local saint.

Nothing remains of the rood groups and the Riding Georges (see Chapter 2 p. 24) which once shared loft space with apostles. Below the wainscoted loft gallery, canopy beams offered space for retelling saint's *Lives*: at Penant Melangell in Wales, for example, the female saint Melangell saves a hare from huntsmen. Few canopy beams survive in Cornwall and so far appear to be saint-free. Hunting scenes, heraldry and fabulous beasts like unicorns and dragons appear at St Buryan, while a naked man is among those running away from fire-breathing dragons at St Ewe. At the Arundell-patronised church of Mawgan in Pydar it is Reynard the Fox and friends who cavort on the south chapel canopy beam now backing the chancel screen.

Moving down to the rail level of the rood loft there are a few carved saints in a proportion of one saint to three secular rail figures as in Brittany, secular figures being fools, strong and wild men, Tudor youths and a naked boy. Surviving saints are Helen at St Ewe, Peter at Luxulyan, Mary at Madron, and an unidentified sawn-down saint wearing long gown and shoes at Veryan. Madron's saint abuts the north wall, probably representing St Mary's chapel, Penzance, and never had secular companions. Other mid-Cornwall screens with Breton secular figures were at St Columb Minor (now lost), Linkinhorne or

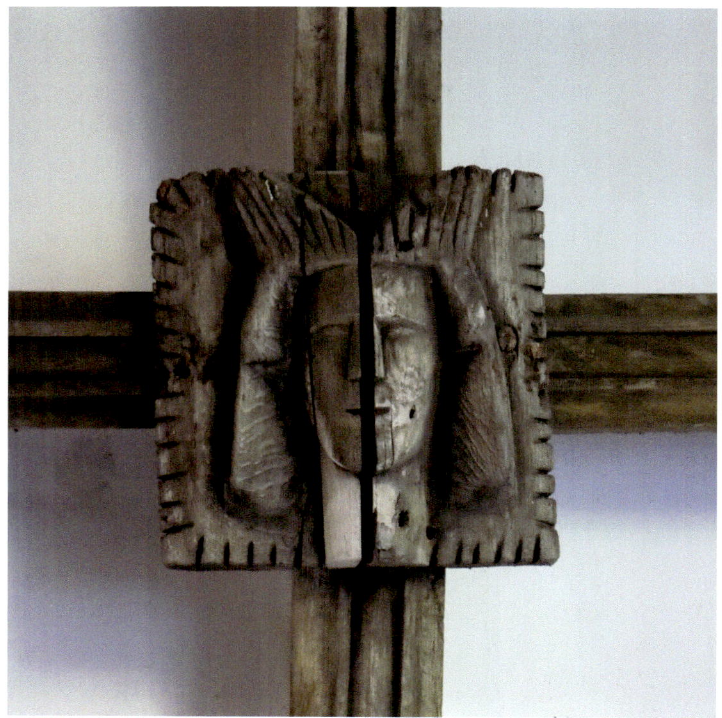

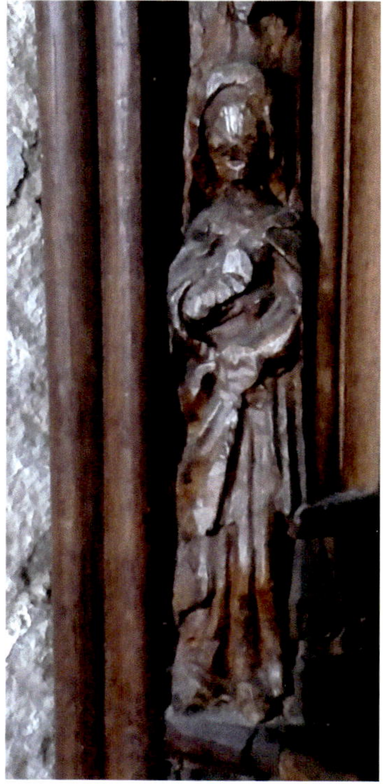

Above left: Laneast. Sidwell roof boss, early sixteenth century. (Photo by Alan Stout)

Above right: Madron. Mary rail figure, early sixteenth century.

North Petherwin (now Cornwall Museum and Art Gallery), Probus and Ruan Lanihorne. At North Petherwin in 1518, three Breton carvers – Peter Papyas, John Oliver and William Wymer – took the rood loft contract, but only their dado survives *in situ.*

Almost half of Cornwall's surviving dadoes have carved panels, a late feature, with painted panels preferred earlier. Triple-headed Trinities appear at Sancreed and Gorran (now a seat back) with a bench-end version at Lansallos, and Passion of Christ symbols on rood loft dadoes at Gwinear and St Levan. The former chapel of St Nicholas, Truro had wainscot figures of apostles.

Bench-ends and Other Woodwork

No local saints are depicted on St Samson Golant's bench-ends, but at St Newlyn East a repaired end may show a headless Newlyn alongside a cockerel, perhaps for St Peter. Newlyn also appears with extra head on a lantern cross now in the church. At Braunton in Devon, St Brannoc is depicted on a bench end as a priest with chalice and ox.

Brittonic saints' symbols occur like Petroc's hunting horn, bell and sword at Little Petherick and Salamon's two fish at St Levan. Eighteenth-century oral traditions state that

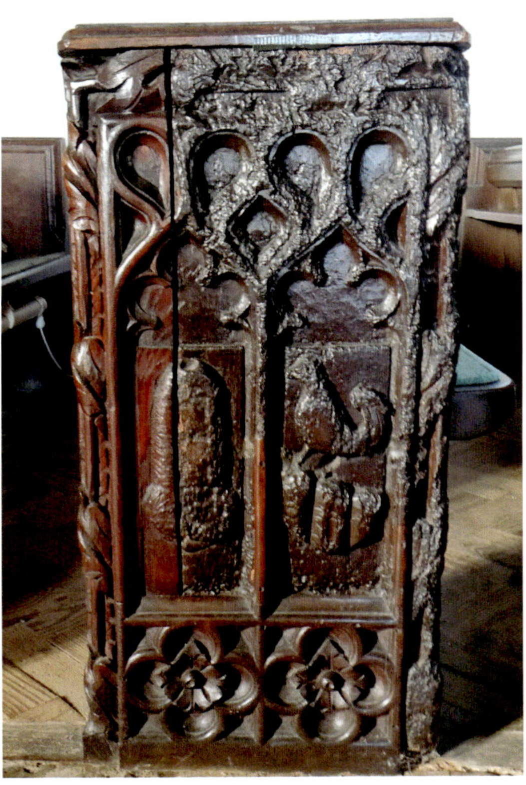
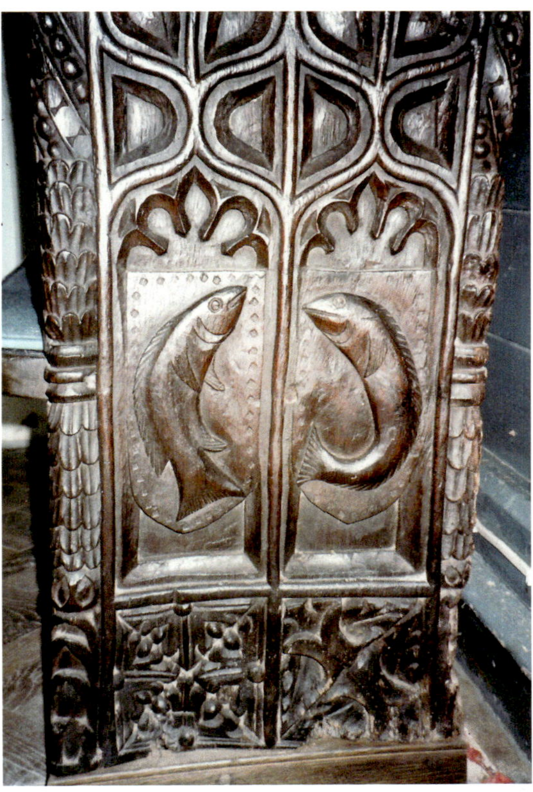

Above left: St Newlyn East. Headless saint and cockerel, bench-end, early to mid-sixteenth century.

Above right: St Levan. Salamon's fish bench-end, early to mid-sixteenth century. (Photo by Bridget Holden)

Salamon caught one fish a day from a coastal rock. One day when two fish were caught three times on one hook, Salamon took them home where he found his sister (either Manacca or Breage) and her children. The children were hungry, but the miraculous fish choked them. Perhaps in the medieval version the saint brought the children back to life. In either case, the bench-end continued to serve its purpose of reminding the parishioners of their local saint, even if the story had become garbled.

A crown over crossed battle-axes at Poughill may represent St Olaf, king of Norway, otherwise why deface the axes on the bench-end? A ship on a bench-end at St Winnow reminds us that seagoing vessels at Fowey and Padstow were named for patronal saints Barry and Petroc just like the children named after their saints at the font.

Most surviving Cornish bench-ends depict the Passion of Christ in shorthand form or sacred monograms of Christ and Mary, although Reynard the Fox and his friends appeared on bench-ends at St Austell, Landulph, North Tamerton, Padstow and formerly St Agnes, Bodmin and St Columb Major. Crucifixion scenes survive at Altarnun, Cornwall and Abbotsham and Woolfardisworthy in Devon. The Zennor mermaid and Poughill pious pelican bench-ends represent Christ's dual nature (half-man and half-God rather than half-man and half-fish) and five wounds. At St Keverne, Christ's resurrection is shown as a shroud and a shroud partly open revealing a man's face. This church also has a pietà paired with a heraldic-style chalice and host.

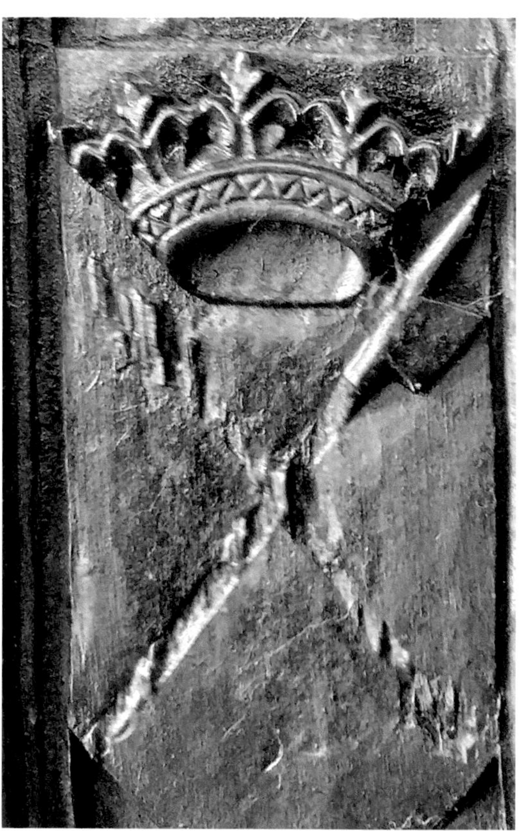

Poughill. Crown and crossed battle-axe(s) of Olaf, early to mid-sixteenth century.

Davidstow's Nativity bench-end celebrated its former guild of St Mary and the donor kneeling below may be the last guild priest, John Langdon (fl. 1546–48). Did he witness the controlled iconoclasm that removed the crib and baby Jesus, but not Mary (who retains some red paint), Joseph or the ox? At St Columb Major a Magi follows a camel.

Apostles were once a popular choice for bench-ends as well as lofts. A surviving bench-end now in the tower of St Austell shows a defaced St John with a chalice and St James the Less with a club, while at St Sampson Golant five apostles – Andrew, Bartholomew, James the Great, Mathias and Thomas – are now part of the pulpit and desks. Stumpy figures at Braddock may be apostles and male and female parishioners. Andrew appears at Tywardreath, while saltire cross-decorated bench-ends occur at Stratton where he was also patron. All four Evangelist symbols appear at Poughill.

The deacon saint at St Sampson Golant is likely to be Lawrence, with gridiron separate; at the mother church of Tywardreath they are shown together. Shorthand bench-end depictions include a wheel and sword for St Katherine at Poughill and wheel at St Winnow. At St Sampson Golant two bench-ends represent the story of George and the dragon. The dragon and St George's banner are on one, while two crowned heads atop castellated towers represent the princess's cowardly parents (see *Churches of Cornwall*, p. 40). A Welsh cupboard at Cotehele and wall paintings in Calstock church tell the story more fully.

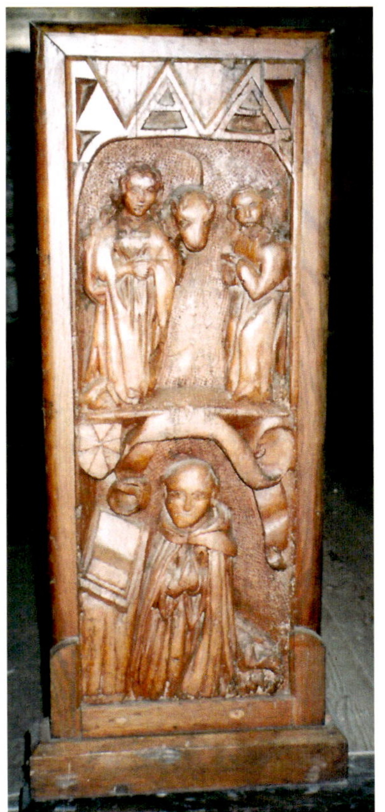

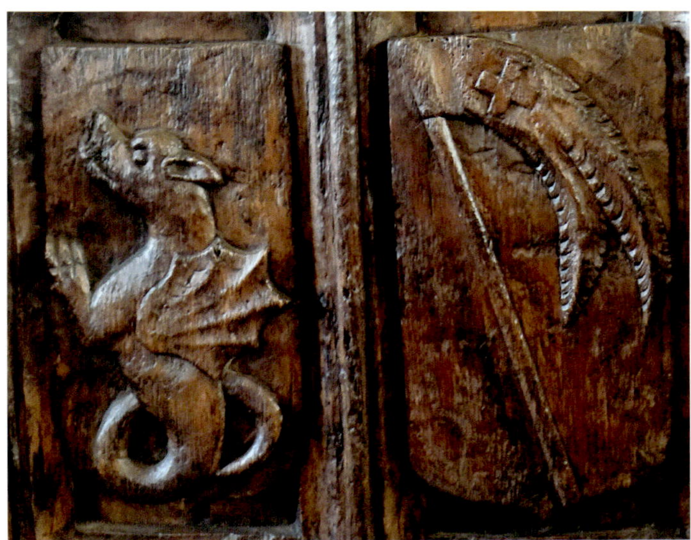

Above: St Sampson Golant. Dragon and George's banner bench-end, early to mid-sixteenth century.

Left: Davidstow. Nativity bench-end with Christ removed, early to mid-sixteenth century. (Photo by Bridget Holden)

Bishops and a priest on bench-ends and prayer desks at Kilkhampton could preserve a memory of John Stanbury (rector 1448–89, bishop of Hereford 1453–74) or represent unrecognised saints. A prayer desk with sloping top at Laneast is badged with the arms of the prior of Launceston, St Peter's cockerel. No figures of saints appear on the handful of misericords that remain in Cornish churches at Bodmin, St Buryan, St Germans or St Just-in-Roseland, unless the last is a winged lion, symbol of St Mark. The St Germans misericord may show the folk tale of Dando and his dogs. Pulpits at Camborne, St Mawgan in Pydar and Padstow have carved Passion symbols rather than saints, while carved or painted Evangelists or saints once filled ogee-headed niches at Launceston St Mary Magdalene or stone pulpit panels at St Mabyn.

Only one carved and painted wooden figure remains, possibly a sixteenth-century St Nicholas at St German, but he looks like an imported figure. No medieval image

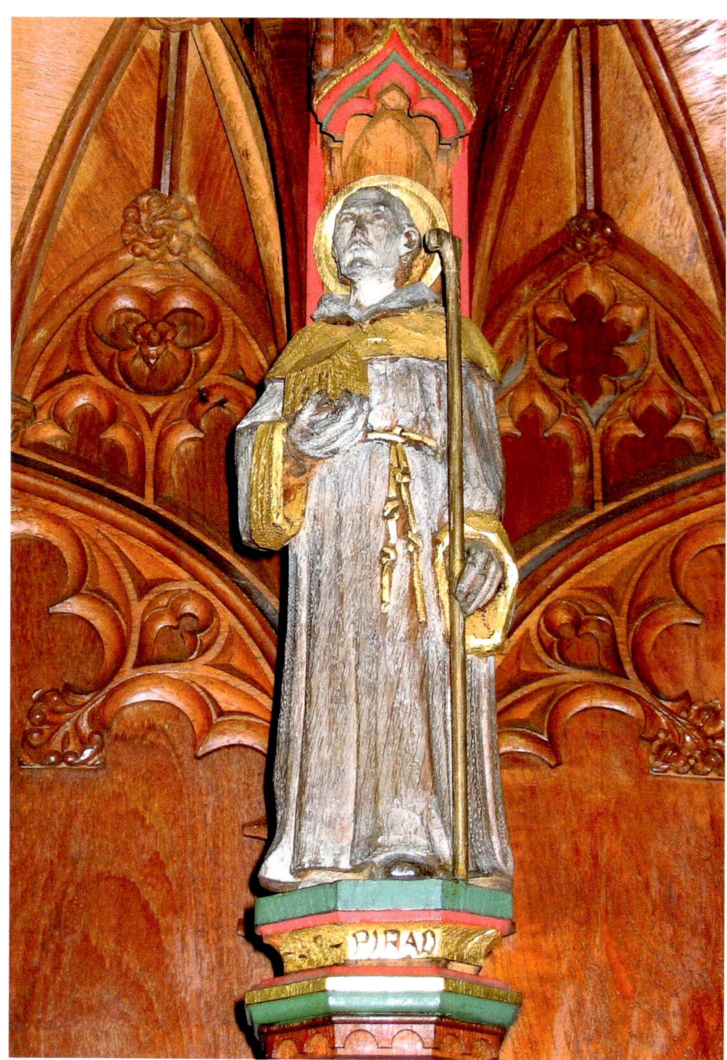

Truro Cathedral. Piran choir-stall carving by Violet Pinwill, 1922–47. (Photo by Helen Wilson)

survives of St Piran, but Violet Pinwill's 1927–44 statue in the Truro Cathedral choir stalls shows a revived interest in local saints then. At the Holy Rood chapel at the Berry in Bodmin in 1505–06, 8*d* was paid for mending the image of St Whyte, probably of wood rather than stone. She was patron saint of Whitchurch Canonicorum in Dorset, where her stone shrine with three mandorla-shaped openings survives. Carved wooden statues of Armel and Mary, commissioned in 1531 for the nave altars at Stratton arrived unpainted in 1538–39 and 1541–42. Their arrival was ill timed, as saints' images were now banned.

Metal and Thread

An unusual gold late sixteenth-century rosary bead in the Victoria and Albert Museum was made as an addition to the early sixteenth-century Langdale rosary. Commissioned by Nicholas Roscarrock, it shows his favourite saint, Endelient, one of the children of Brychan, with her cow, martyr's palm and holy well. Based at Trentinney in St Endellion parish, Endelient lived a very austere life, consuming only milk. When the lord of that place killed her cow, King Arthur had him slain. A gold iconographic fifteenth-century ring of St Margaret, patron saint of childbirth, from Linkinhorne is now displayed in the Cornwall Museum and Art Gallery.

Silver-gilt, latten (a brass-like metal) and pewter were among the metals used for saints' statues. St Michael's Mount once had three silver-gilt images of Michael, while a twelfth-century pewter crucified Christ with a high tin content survives at Ludgvan. Only a paten from Morval and a chalice from Braddock survive of medieval church

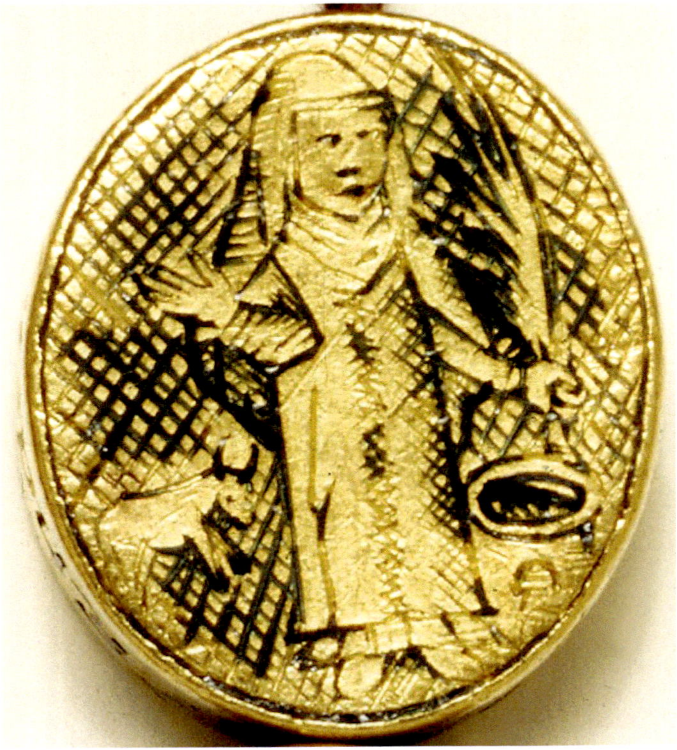

Langdale Rosary. Endelient rosary bead, late sixteenth century. (V&A image, by permission)

plate, with the former depicting Christ's head imprinted on Veronica's veil. Saints appear occasionally on memorial brasses and seals, including the clumsily restored image of St Michael on Oto Trenwith's 1460s brass at St Ives and an Evangelist eagle at Saltash. Jesus's mercy was sought on brasses at Crowan and Sithney and St Mary's help at Crowan.

Bells rang out against thunder and fifty-two medieval bells survive in Cornwall, often with Christ's sacred IHC monogram. King Alfred was invoked at St Enodoc, and Petroc's name added to St Anna at Little Petherick, the only Brittonic saint's name now on a bell. Today Mary is called on when bells are rung in six Cornish churches, Margaret four times, Anna, John, Michael, Nicholas and Thomas twice, and Andrew, Barnabas, Christopher, Clement, Gabriel, George, Katherine, Mary Magdalene, Paul, Peter and Raphael once.

Cotehele House chapel, uniquely in Cornwall, preserves an altar dorsal or back of purple velvet with embroidered figures of Christ and the twelve apostles, Paul substituting for Judas. This and a black wool frontal are badged with the arms of Sir Piers Edgcumbe, knight, and his first wife, Jane Durnford, suggesting a date between 1493 and *c.* 1521. The figures on the black frontal are Roche, Antony, John the Baptist, Michael, Erasmus, Sebastian and the prophet Jeremiah (some being illustrated in *The Antiquaries Journal*, 2024). On 4 December 1553, when Lady Katharine Edgcumbe, Sir Piers' second wife and former lady-in-waiting to Anne of Cleves, made her will, she left a year's wages to two Cotehele chaplains, including her old Welsh chaplain William Jenkins.

5. Glazed Saints

Seven Years a Hermit – The St Neot Window

The first window you see on entering St Neot church dates from 1530 and depicts the *Life* of St Neot. Rightly famed for its stained glass, St Neot is Cornwall's second-largest parish and its saint was claimed by the Saxons as well as the Cornish. Like Altarnun and St Cleer, the parish includes a vast tract of Bodmin Moor and was a centre of late medieval tin working and processing. St Neot's church town was on the old Bodmin–Liskeard road.

Unlike the stone, wood and metal from which many saints were made, all glass had to be imported. As late as *c.* 1470, St Kew and St Winnow received ready-made Exeter stained-glass panels packed in straw, but from 1491 there were alternative local glaziers at Bodmin. Corpus Vitrearum locations, noted on the plan of St Neot church, are used below to explain the movement of glass around St Neot church.

The 1530 window of St Neot's *Life* may be the work of the Bodmin glazier John Hewet. It is much restored, but the content is little altered apart from the date, now mistakenly reading 1528. Paid for by the young men of St Neot parish, this ambitious window lies opposite the south entrance (n7). Episodes from the twelfth- or thirteenth-century *Life* of St Neot created a remarkable comic book in glass. Twelve scenes in three rows can be 'read' from left to right, row by row. To aid the literate there are simple Latin explanatory scrolls below each scene beginning with the word '*hic*' or 'here'. Short enough to be read out loud, not all are now decipherable. Backgrounds of imaginary city walls and turrets have skies of alternating blue, green or red, indoor scenes have cobbled floors, while outdoor ones take place in yellow-stain meadows with grass and curious three-petalled flowers.

The first scene at top left shows the Saxon Neot handing over his crown and sceptre to a younger brother, witnessed by a servant. In the second scene Neot is shown kneeling (halo lost) and taking his vows on an open book before a monk. The abbot of Glastonbury, a clerk with holy water bucket and another monk look on.

In the third scene the action shifts to Neot's seven years' sojourn as a hermit in Cornwall. Neot, still in Glastonbury blue, saves a doe from a huntsman while reading his psalter and bathing his feet in a circular well. Original glass shows a kneeling deer and young huntsman, wearing a fashionable green-sleeved tunic and slashed hose, handing Neot his hunting horn. According to legend this horn was later given by Neot to St Petroc's church, Bodmin. The *Life* tells us that Neot wore a hair shirt and immersed himself up to his neck while reading his psalter. In the fourth scene three fish now swim in the well, with its gargoyle overflow. In the legend the angel (with 1820s replacement head) warns Neot to take only one fish a day.

The second row begins with Neot, sick in bed, asking his servant Barry (Barrius in Latin) to bring him his daily fish. Foolish Barry decides to takes two fish, grilling one

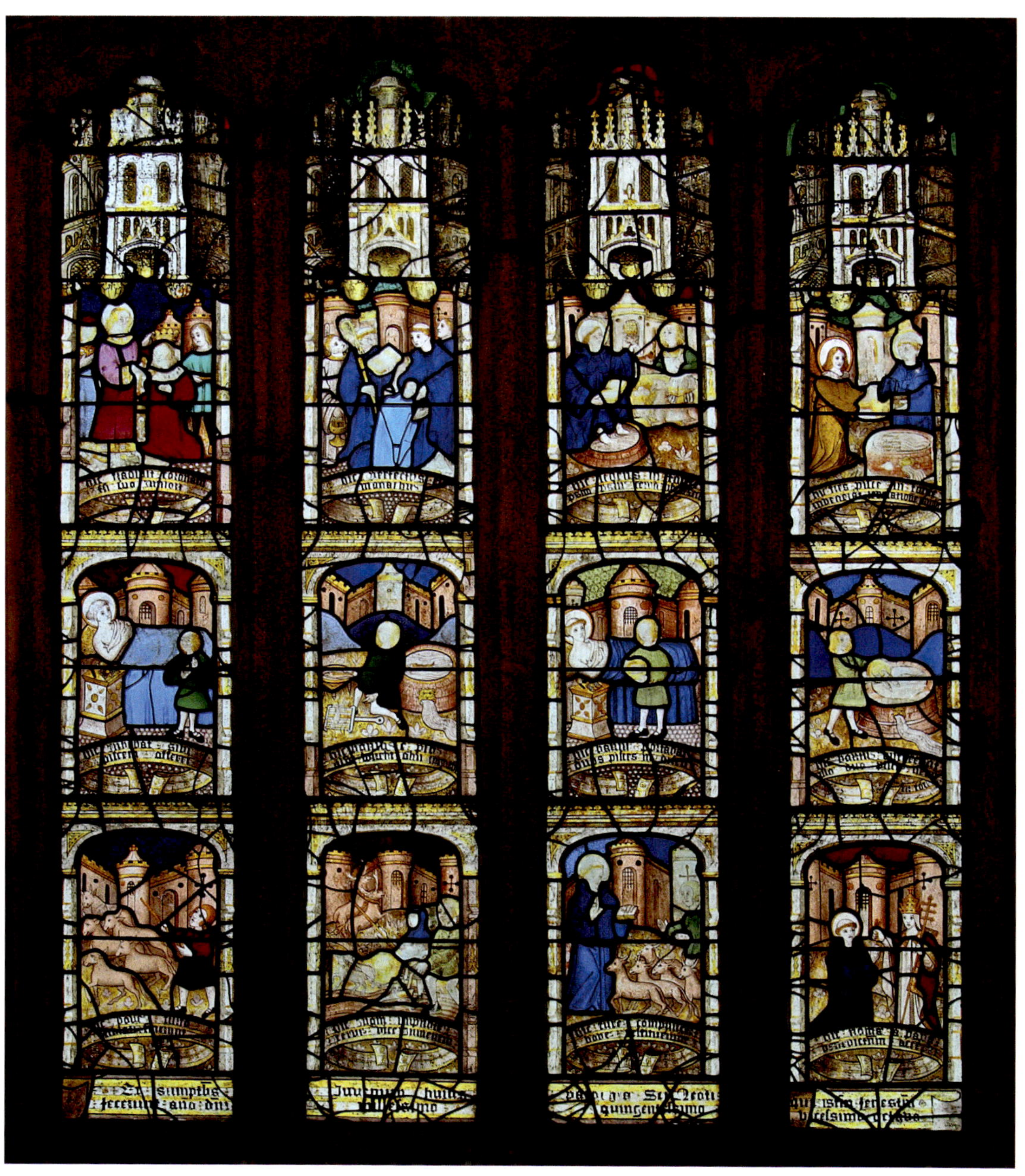

St Neot. Neot window-type, 1530 (n7). (Photo by Eric Berry)

and boiling the other to tempt his master to eat. In the next scene Neot orders Barry to return both fish to the well where they miraculously revive. These popular scenes were repeated in nearby roof bosses (see p. 56) while the much-restored Neot's well still lies half a mile from the church. Holy wells containing fish are a common element in folk beliefs in Wales and Ireland.

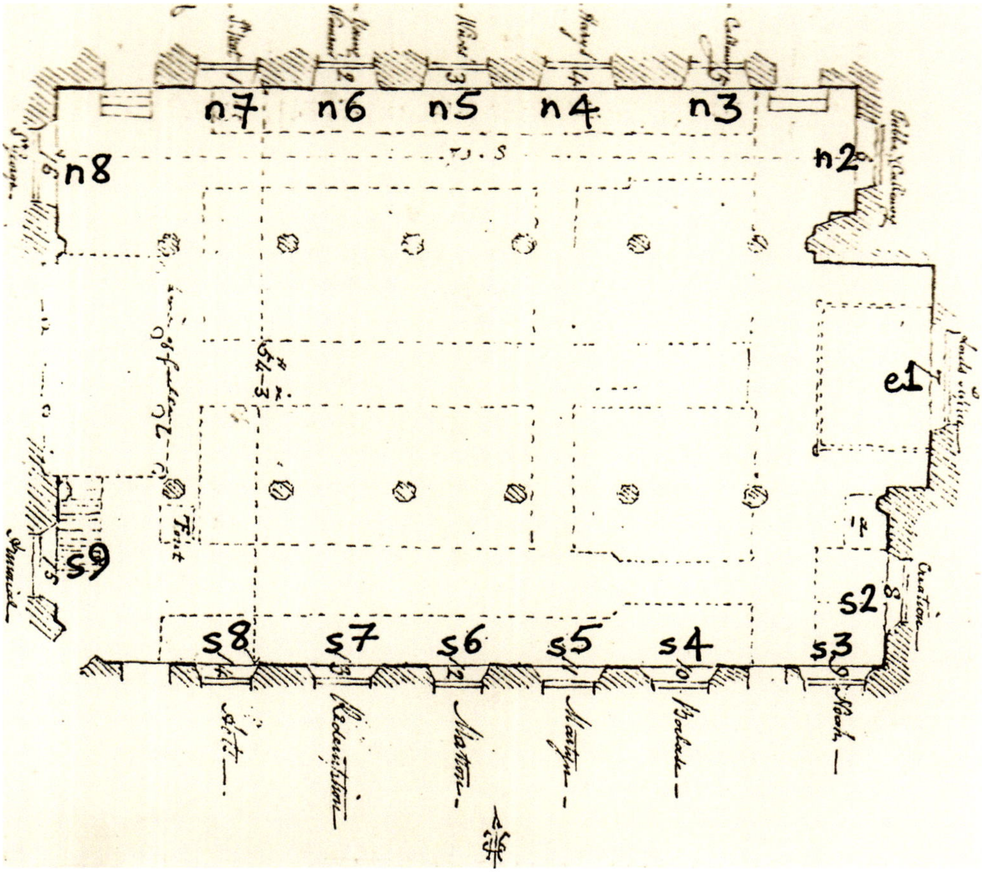

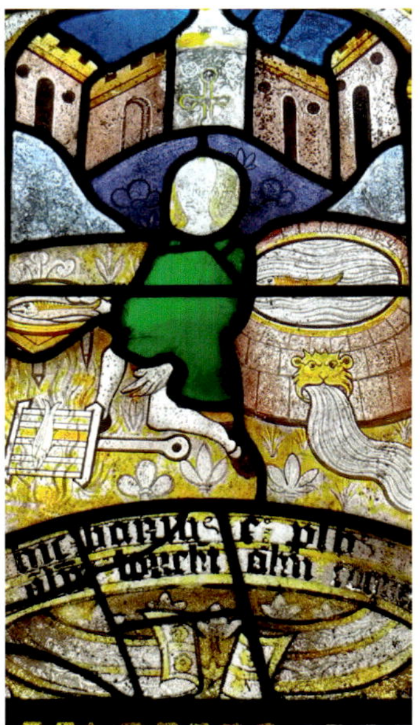

Above: St Neot. Corpus Vitrearum window locations. (1830 Hedgeland base plan by kind permission of the Royal Institution of Cornwall)

Left: St Neot. Barry boils one fish and grills another, 1530 (n7). (Photo by Piers Kent)

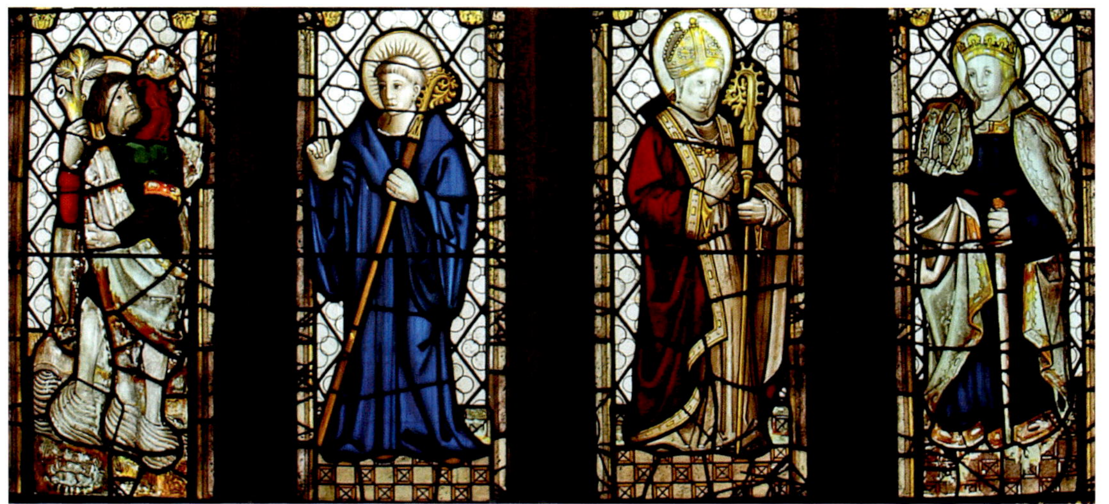

St Neot. St Neot, 1820s, with saints Christopher, Leonard and Katherine, 1500s (s4). (Photo by Eric Berry)

In the final row a thief steals the saint's oxen, originally a plough team of four but restored as five. Four stags now come to plough Neot's lands, because he saved their doe from the huntsmen. A similar scene of stags ploughing from the *Life* of St Robert of Knaresborough can be seen at Morley church, Derbyshire, originally in Dale Abbey, and stag ploughing featured in the sixteenth-century play performed at Playing Place in Kea parish. Only St Neot's ploughman with fourteenth-century-style head coif, hooded boy, plough and two lower stags are original. The eleventh scene shows the return of the oxen and in the last Neot kneels before the Pope. By ending with Neot's pilgrimage to Rome, the young men's group avoided any awkwardness about the saint's burial place, while stressing his international importance.

There are notable omissions from the story as told in glass. For example, Neot's cure of King Alfred, which led to Neot's bones being stolen, the attempted theft of the saint's shoe by a fox, and the roofless Crow Pound where Neot reputedly coralled crows during service time. The window also fails to show Neot's diminutive stature as depicted on the front façade of Crowland Abbey, Lincolnshire. Childlike or dwarfish stature is conferred instead on St Neot's hapless servant Barry, probably intended for the patron saint of Fowey, depicted in a short green tunic and black shoes.

Another 1500s image of Neot appeared in the Lady Chapel in the Borlase family window (s4), showing that local patron saints were acceptable there. Although an 1820s reconstruction, it is probably not too different from the original.

Other Local and Glazed Saints at St Neot

Images of over thirty and perhaps more than forty different saints once filled the windows of St Neot. Three west windows were lost in the great storm of 1703, so it is unclear whether they held single figures or saints' *Lives*. The missing tower window might have contained fourteenth-century glass. Possible subjects for the lost 1500s south-west window or *c.* 1531 north-west window are St Anne and a second St Luke as saints of parish chapels or

St Willow of Lanteglos-by-Fowey, whose two companions appear in the north aisle. The north-west window was probably paid for by the wives of the eastern part of St Neot parish.

Ten surviving saints at St Neot are female and twenty male, although three females only appear high up in tracery lights. In contrast to the more sophisticated single-phase schemes of All Saints in North Street, York, Fairford in Gloucestershire or King's College chapel, Cambridge, the glazing at St Neot's church in Cornwall was done at four or more different times, and was more typical of parish churches as a whole with some duplication of saints. Closely related to the church building programme, identifiable glazing episodes run from the mid-fifteenth century chancel east window (e1 and s7) through the 1480s south chapel 1500s south aisle to the 1520s–30s north aisle.

The north side was the local side and appearing with St Neot are seven more Brittonic saints. International saints populated the sunnier south side and chancel, with another small pocket in the north chapel and start of the north aisle, attributable partly to Devon donors. Images of Christ and Mary were sprinkled throughout the church as devotional magnets, with iconoclasm before 1651 targeted on these figures.

The first local saint on the north side was Lallu of Menheniot, who originally appeared in the north chapel (n3). Although 1820s work, Lallu's religious habit, book and cross staff is likely to be close to the original and mirrored Neot in the Lady Chapel opposite. He and St German, who had a local cult at St Germans, were clumsily combined with part of a crucifixion scene and St Stephen from the north-east window (n2) in the 1820s and later moved to the south aisle (s7).

John Calway, gentleman of Menheniot and Devon, was the donor and had a son Lallowe named after the saint. In 1426–1581 there was a Lallu's guild at Menheniot and St Lalluwy well, a relatively modern structure, stands down the street from Menheniot church. Noted in 1513 as the saint's well, this probably had a stone well-house then. The original Lallu window (n3) included another crucified Christ, perhaps signifying a northern Jesus chapel where Friday Masses were said.

In the 1528 window paid for by the wives of the western part of the parish (n. 5), St Mabyn, one of the daughters of Brychan, was chosen. Little original glass survives, but depiction as a

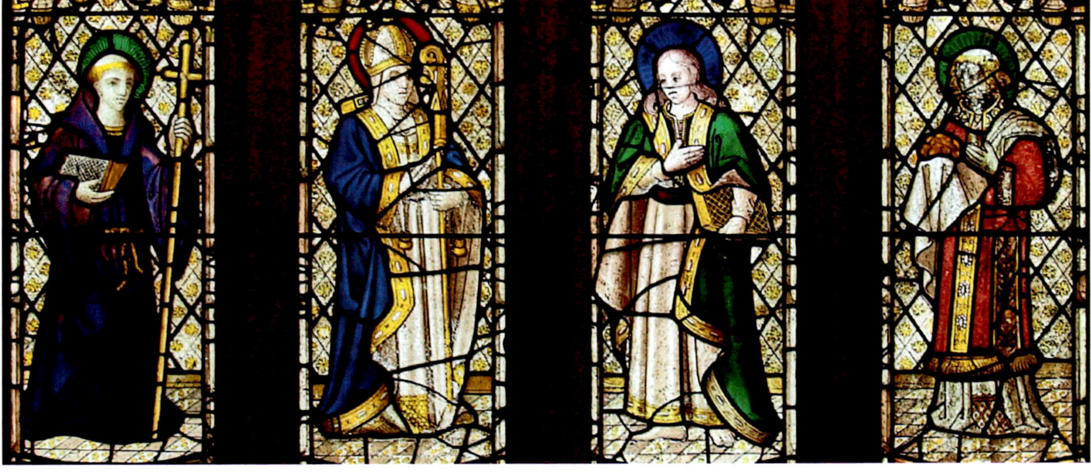

St Neot. St Lallu, 1820s, with saints German, John and Stephen, 1520s (n2-3 now s7). (Photo by Eric Berry)

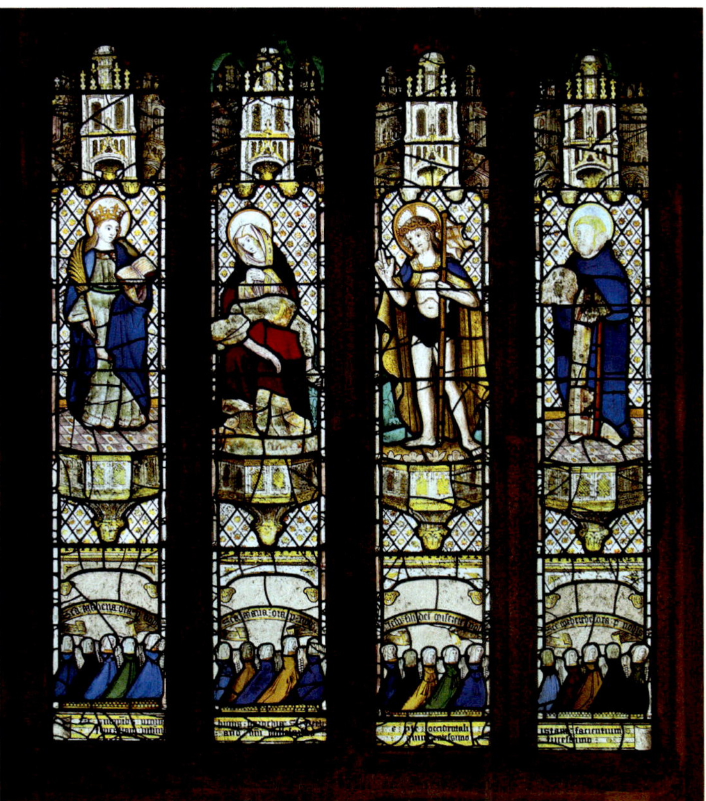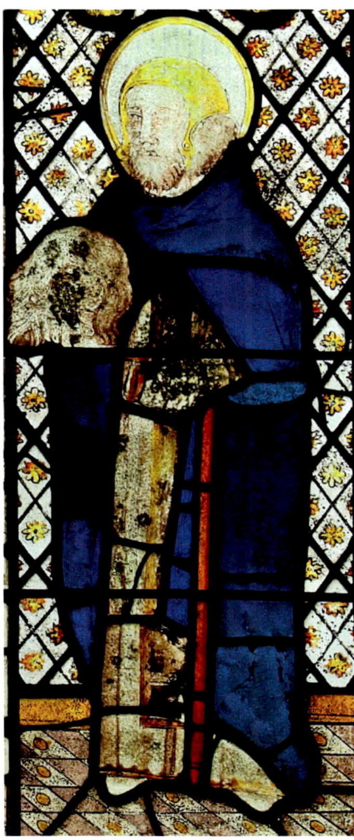

Above left and above right: St Neot. St Mabyn, Pietà, Christ and St Meubred, 1528 and detail of latter (n5). (Photo by Eric Berry)

martyr with palm and book was normal for female saints at this time. We know that Mabyn's late medieval cult was enlivened by a hymn noting her twenty-three holy siblings, and that St Paul's well, half a mile north of St Mabyn church, may once have been dedicated to her.

The wives' second local saint was Meubred of Cardinham. Distinctively shown as a hermit with yellow head coif and a long blue cloak over an alb, Meubred holds a second head, disfigured with dirt, and a staff. Noted as a martyr in 1473, by 1478 Meubred was said to be the son of King Colrogus of Ireland. He had two holy companions, Manac and Willow, patrons of Lanreath and Lanteglos-by-Fowey who shared his feast day on the Thursday before Whitsun. A chapel over a well a short distance from Cardinham church was probably associated with Meubred, who was also once depicted in glass at his own church of Cardinham. Generations of the Wills family were christened Meubred at Cardinham and in 1478 William of Worcester may have met the wife of one.

A trio of male local bishop saints – Petroc, Clair and Manac, companion of Meubred – appear in the next window (n6), with All Saints. This window was paid for by the sisters of the parish in 1529, a young women or maidens' group. Here Petroc wears a green chasuble, a white-and-gold patterned surplice and plentiful gold rings over white leather gloves, with a crosier in his right gloved hand. Although often depicted as a hermit (see p. 50), perhaps a bishop was more impressive for St Neot folk and also advertised the skills of the glovers' of Petroc's Bodmin guild.

Petroc's and Neot's *Lives* shared episodes like royal abdication, becoming a monk, evicting resident local saints, going on pilgrimage to Rome, eating only fish, and saving a deer, but Petroc outdid Neot in each case. Thus Petroc was the son of a Welsh king, studied in Ireland for twenty years, ousted two Cornish saints Bishop Wethenoc at Padstow and Goran at Bodmin, extended his Rome pilgrimage to Jerusalem and India, lived on one fish for seven years there, came back to Cornwall to kill a serpent, created a well, lived a hermit's life with twelve disciples in a wilderness at Little Petherick and moved to Bodmin to die (see pp. 23, 30-1, 50). Other sources claim Petroc died at Padstow, his remains being later taken to Bodmin, which is more likely. The name Petroc was one of the most popular of Cornish Christian names not surprisingly as Petroc and Michael were joint patron saints of medieval Cornwall.

The second bishop saint in the 1529 window is Clair, patron of St Cleer, though only his gloved hands, rings and cloak lining are original. Clair was probably a distinct Cornish saint with the finest of all Cornish well-chapels a short distance from St Cleer church (see p. 17). Built as a giant granite shrine and carefully restored in 1864, it has three open arcades, a back wall with lower round arches and a paved floor. Nothing is known of this Clair's life beyond his depiction as a bishop.

Manac, the third bishop, was noted in 1478 as an 'Irish' bishop, companion to Meubred and Willow, and buried in Lanreath church. By this time, he shared church patronage at Lanreath with the better-known Dunstan as part of a process of intended local saint replacement. In a final local twist, All Saints in the fourth light of the sisters' window was fancifully reinterpreted and restored in the 1820s as King Brychan, father of the twenty-four children.

The rest of St Neot's glazing focuses on international saints, but there is a reference to the cult of the Holy Rood in the 1480s Creation window. Adam's death-bed scene shows Seth planting seeds from Eden in Adam's nostrils and mouth. In the background the Christ child can be seen in the branches of the tree which grew from these and later provided timber

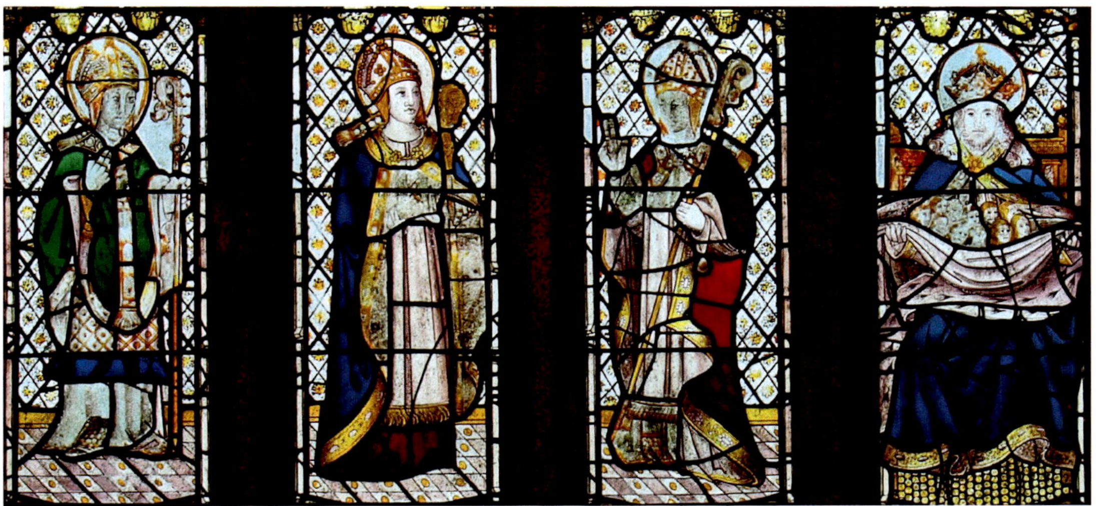

St Neot. Saints Petroc, Clair, Manac and All Saints, 1529 (n6). (Photo by Eric Berry)

for Christ's crucifix (s2). The centre of the cult in Cornwall was the chapel of the Holy Rood at the Berry, Bodmin. The adjacent Noah window (s3) probably continued the story up to the building of Solomon's temple as the first day's play of the *Cornish Ordinalia* does. Old Testament windows at Great Malvern offer parallels, but no reference to the Holy Rood.

Local and International Saints Depicted in Cornish Churches

Windows depicting Brittonic patron saints were once common in Cornish churches, as shown by St Winnow. This church has the best collection of glazed saints after St Neot, but no indication of a glazing scheme. Eight and a half saints of *c.* 1470 date from at least two windows crowd into two tiers of the east window of the south chantry chapel. The saints are George, the Virgin and Child, Christopher, Michael (a St Michael Penkevil–Carminow connection), an unidentifiable half-bishop, a bishop, probably Winnoc, Sidwell, Mary from an Annunciation, and Leonard. Winnoc is depicted as a bishop with crosier and a rich red chasuble with gold fleur de lys decoration.

Lost local patron saints in glass included Meubred at Cardinham noted above, Columb and Feoc. Before the accidental gunpowder explosion of 1676 caused by schoolboys at St Columb Major church, a female Columb was depicted in glass and stone with her dove. Boys and girls were baptised Columb in the 1540s and in 1570, such gender confusion being not uncommon with local saints and exacerbated by the existence of a male St Columba. At Feock a bonneted image of Feoc in a south aisle window could be read as either male or female, while a fragment with hand and book at Lamorran could be St Moran or any bishop saint.

Golant people in the 1500s paid for an image of Samson for their mother church of Tywardreath and the Saxon abbess St Etheldreda of Ely still appears in stained glass at St Sidwell's church, Laneast. At St Agnes there was once a glazed *Life* of the church's international patron saint. Although mostly destroyed in the Civil War, a scene of St Agnes in a Rome prison remained. From this fragment a local legend was spun starting with St Agnes's escape to Cornwall as we saw at the start of the first chapter.

Locating stained-glass international saints within the church is problematic, with the exception of St Neot's. Cornish chancel windows often showed crucifixion scenes as at Cotehele Chapel and St Winnow, with suggestive fragments in east windows at Altarnun, Creed, Lamorran and Laneast. At Mullion the east window subject was the adoration of the magi and at St Neot the founders of the Christian church, Peter and Paul, were paired with Christ showing his wounds and the pilgrimage saint James the Great. There were two crucifixion windows at St Neot, the north-east window (n2 partly moved to s7) and a window abutting the rood loft in the south aisle where a side altar was once located (s5). In both cases Stephen and his stones filled the fourth light. A second crucified Christ survives at Laneast, but its original location is unclear.

Annunciation scenes are found over east windows as tracery lights at Cotehele and St Neot and in the south-east chapel with a coronation of the Virgin at Lanteglos-by-Fowey. Another Annunciation was over a Holy Kindred window by St Neot's south entrance (s8), perhaps marking the site of the churching seat for mothers returning to church a month after childbirth. The Virgin and child (s5) appeared here with her half-sisters Mary Salome and Mary Cleophas and their children with a fourth panel showing a Warning to Sabbath Breakers. This and Mary Salome are now at the Cornwall Museum and Art Gallery. A further

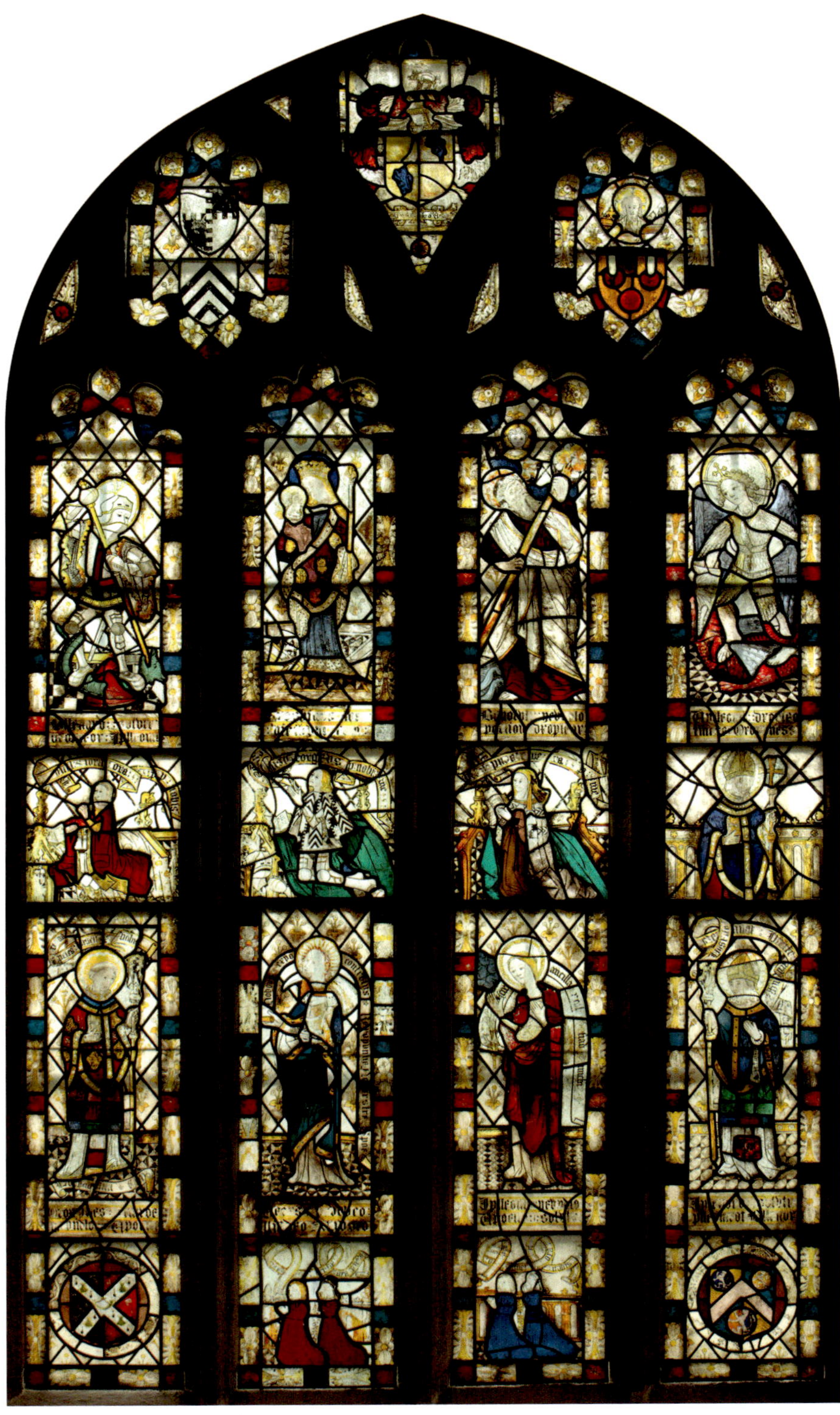

St Winnow. South-east window saints, *c.* 1470. (Photo by Mark Charter)

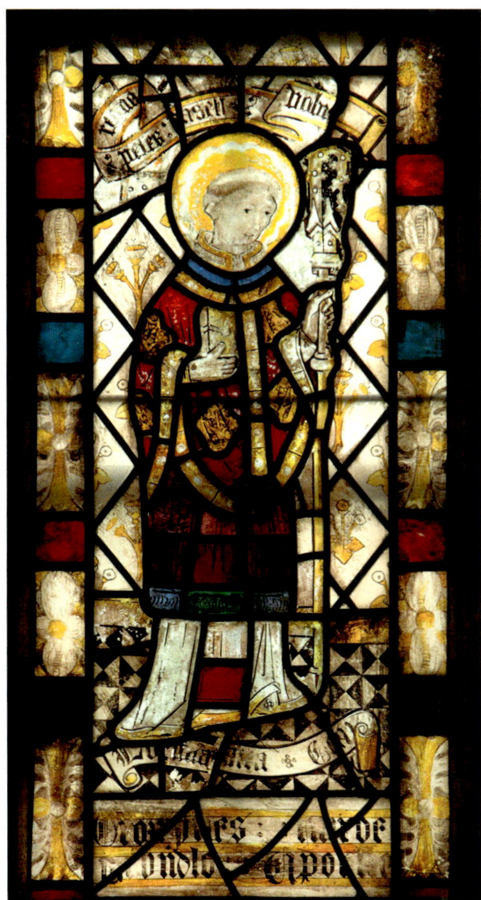 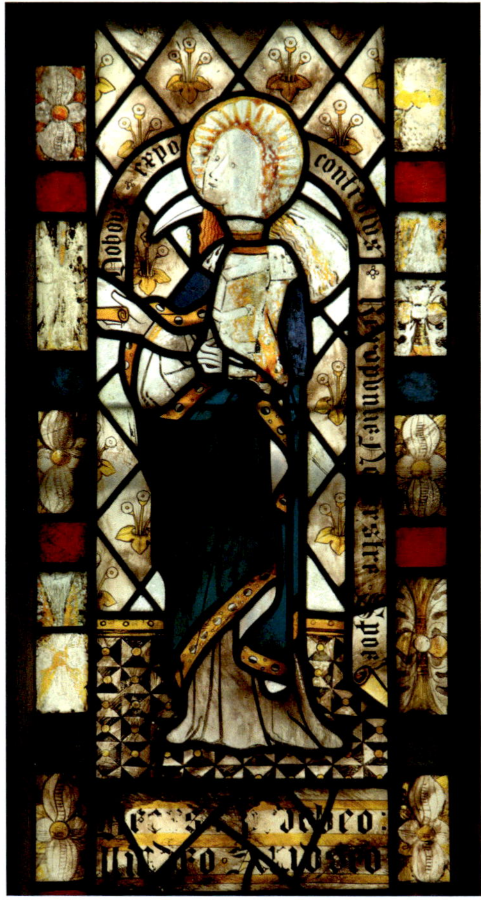

Above left: St Winnow. St Winnoc, *c.* 1470. (Photo by Mark Charter)

Above right: St Winnow. St Sidwell, *c.* 1470. (Photo by Mark Charter)

Below: Lamorran. Bishop fragment and Golgotha, turned on side, medieval. (Photo by Alan Stout)

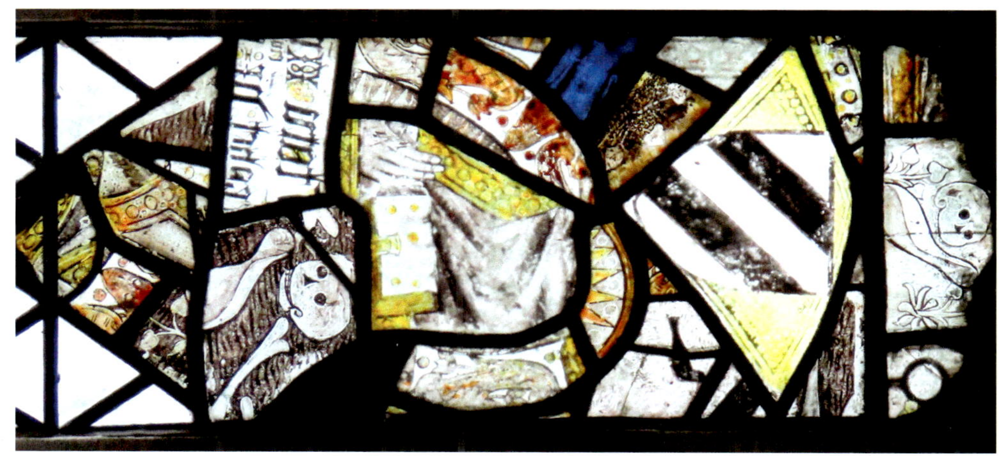

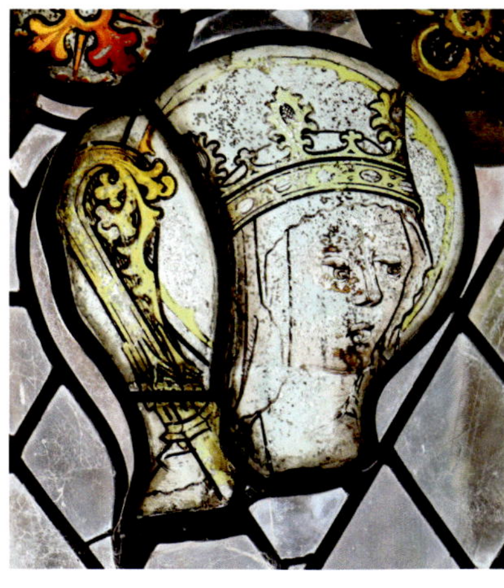

Laneast. Etheldreda, medieval. (Photo by Alan Stout)

six Annunciations are represented only by heads or a single figure at Breage, St Breock, St Enoder, Quethiock, Sheviock, Sithney and St Winnow, while displaced Nativity panels in the north-east window at St Kew suggest a missing Life of the Virgin window there.

Resurrection scenes of Christ stepping out of his tomb occur in tracery lights over St Kew's south-east Jesse window and St Neot's *Life* of St George window (s7) while a soldier sleeps over Creed's south-east window. In Lanteglos-by-Camelford's Lady Chapel sophisticated tracery lights show female witnesses of the Resurrection, while Christ's Passion and Resurrection can be seen in the 1480s north-east window at St Kew and formerly in east and south-east windows at Michaelstow.

James the Great occurs at St Neot and St Sampson Golant and with other apostles in the south aisle at Lanteglos-by-Camelford and St Neot, while at Altarnun apostles Creed windows were once on the north side. Katherine, a popular female saint, can be found at St Kew, St Neot and Cotehele sponsored by Lady Katherine Edgcumbe, Christopher at Laneast, Lanteglos-by-Camelford and St Neot and Leonard twice at St Neot. A *Life* of St George in twelve scenes was formerly in the south aisle at St Neot (s7 now n8) and once mirrored the *Life of St Neot* window in the north aisle. Probably funded by a local guild of St George, it shows George fighting the Gauls, his beheading and resurrection as St Mary's knight (see p. 5), slaying the dragon and subsequent tortures culminating in a second beheading. In scene eight George is being ridden by the Emperor's son in a parody of scene four where George fights the dragon. Another St George image was once in the north chapel at St Neot with Lallu (n3).

Anne teaches the Virgin to read in Cotehele chapel (see p. 20), Anthony and his pig are at St Sampson Golant, Barbara, Gregory, Helen, John the Baptist and Margaret at St Neot, and the Trinity at Egloskerry. A mitre in St Martin-by-Looe's east window might relate to their patron saint and continental-style roundels at St Kew show Ambrose, Augustine, Lawrence and Michael.

Saints like St John the Evangelist had a group identity as crucifixion attendant, apostle and Evangelist. Evangelists at St Neot are in the south aisle (s6) as are their symbols at Creed, St Kew, Lanteglos-by-Camelford, Poundstock and St Tudy. St John the Baptist's lamb, the *Agnes Dei*, can still be seen at St Kew and Truro. Sacred monograms and Christ's passion symbols are also commonly found.

6. Painted Saints

Murals

At Breage church, near Helston, there are nine late medieval paintings of saints and a fragment of a tenth in the main body of the church of late fifteenth-century date. A late sixteenth-century text overlies other painting north of the screen and in the south aisle, with Victorian stencil painting in the south chapel. This is the best Cornwall can offer by way of medieval wall paintings, similar to other West Country counties but not comparable to East Anglia, where survival is much better.

Found during the 1890 restoration of the church, saints are painted in earth colours and black with more colour for St Christopher, who was perhaps shown in profile originally. Seven paintings are on the north side and three on the south occupying a limited 'canvas' between three-light Perpendicular aisle windows. Eastern splays of the windows were also used. A fragmentary tenth painting over the north door is squashed between Christopher

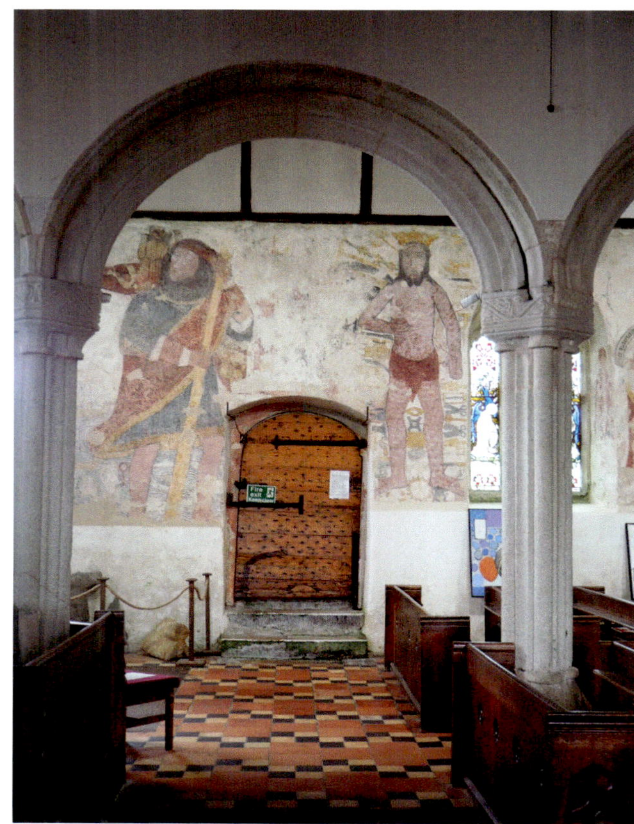

Breage. St Christopher and
Warning to Sabbath Breakers,
late fifteenth century.
(Photo by Nina Hocking)

and the Warning to Sabbath Breakers (St Sunday). It has its own frame and the surviving scroll and paint suggest this was an enthroned St Mary image, as found on lantern crosses.

Enough survives to suggest parallels with the St Neot glass. Breage's north aisle was where local saints and patrons of nearby churches were honoured, the south being left for better-known international saints with pilgrimage credentials.

St Corentin, patron saint of Cury, one of three Breage daughter chapels, occupies a prominent position on the north wall. A smaller figure than Christopher, and set lower down, but larger than the window splay figures, Corentin wears an ochre gown with a red cloak and raises his right hand in blessing, while his left holds a rather large crosier. Overhead a black-lettered scroll reads '*St Quorentine ora* [*pro nobis*]', translating as 'St Corentin pray for us'. The one unusual feature of this painting is the large fish painted in an upright position just to the right of the saint's feet.

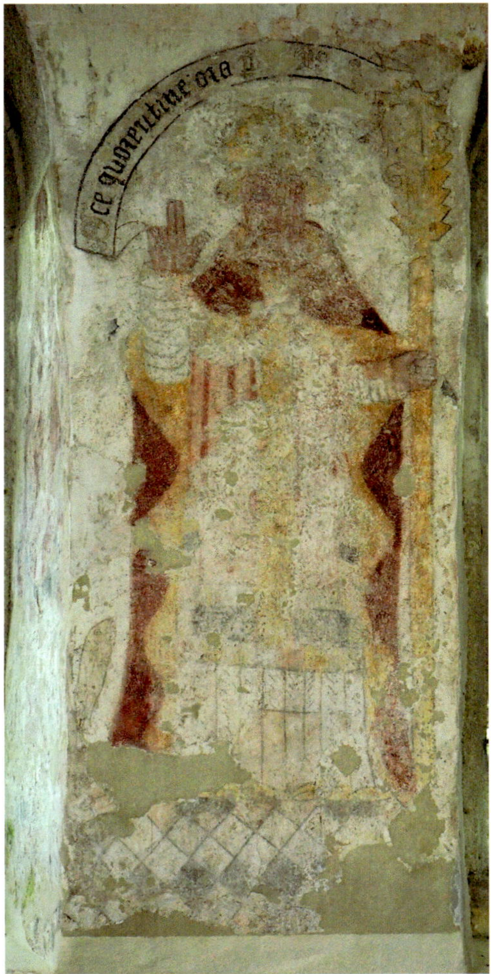
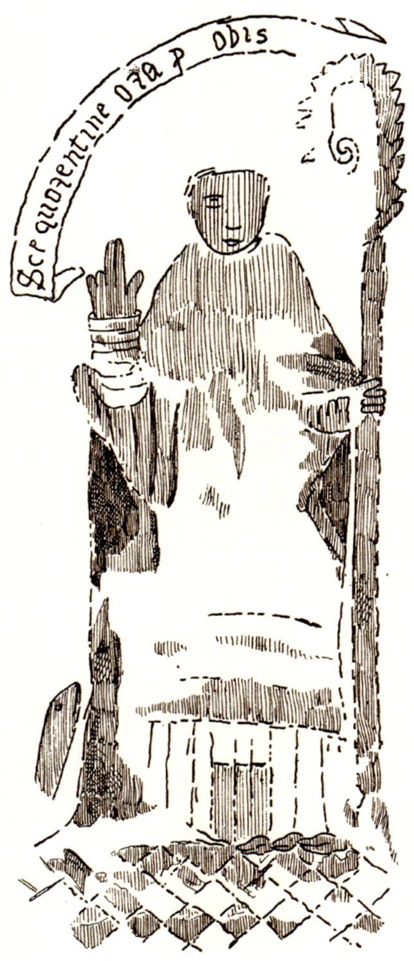

Above left and above right: Breage. Images of St Corentin and fish, late fifteenth century. (Photo by Nina Hocking; plate 4, *JRIC*, XIV, 1901)

Corentin, or Cury in his pet form, was first noted as a Breton saint in the late ninth-century *Life* of Winwaloe, and by the 1230s was described in Brittany as a hermit and first bishop of Cornouaille in Brittany. According to Breton legend, he dwelt by a stream and lived off a single miraculous fish, but only by taking one slice a day. After feeding the king of Cornuaille's hunting party, a courtier cut a second slice. Corentin then had to heal his fish and advised it to vanish. The wall painting at Breage shows that stories of St Corentin and his magic fish were well known in Cornwall; Cury John, who mustered there in 1569, was named after the saint.

St Hilary is shown as a bishop and identified by a label below his feet in the window splay west of Corentin. He was patron of the nearby parish of St Hilary, including Marazion with links to St Michael's Mount. Hilary was a fourth-century bishop of Poitiers

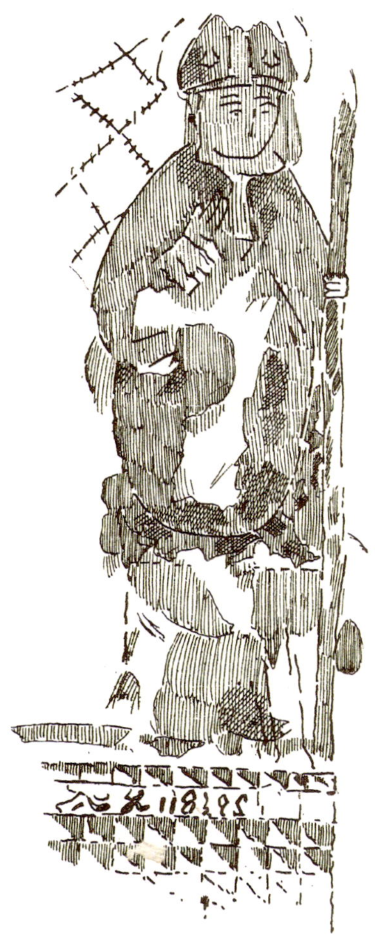

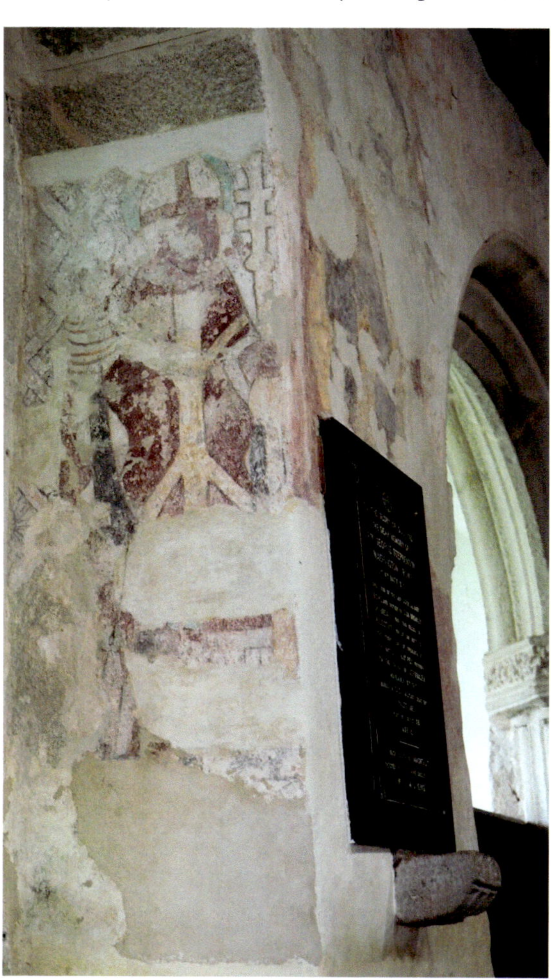

Above left: Breage. Hilary, late fifteenth century. (Plate 3, *JRIC*, XIV, 1901)

Above right: Breage. Saints Augustine and Michael with statue bracket, late fifteenth century. (Photo by Nina Hocking)

and a familiar figure in French, Breton and Welsh churches. The next window splay to the east shows a figure likely to be St Augustine of Canterbury with St Michael next to him. Binnerton manor chapel in Crowan parish was dedicated to Augustine and had links with Breage church. The now faceless winged figure of Michael, patron of St Michael's Mount, has a raised sword, the dragon dead at his feet. Missing Brittonic saints are Breaca, Germoc and Winwaloe, representing the patron saint and daughter chapels at Germoe and Gunwalloe. Perhaps these were lost when the north transept was created *c.* 1530.

The south-aisle paintings show Henry VI next to the door, and international saints Giles and Thomas Becket in window splays further east. Henry VI is shown with a crown, sceptre and ermine-edged robe and was credited with curing Cornishmen of fever and plague, Cornish pilgrims visited Henry's Windsor shrine as late as the 1540s and probably

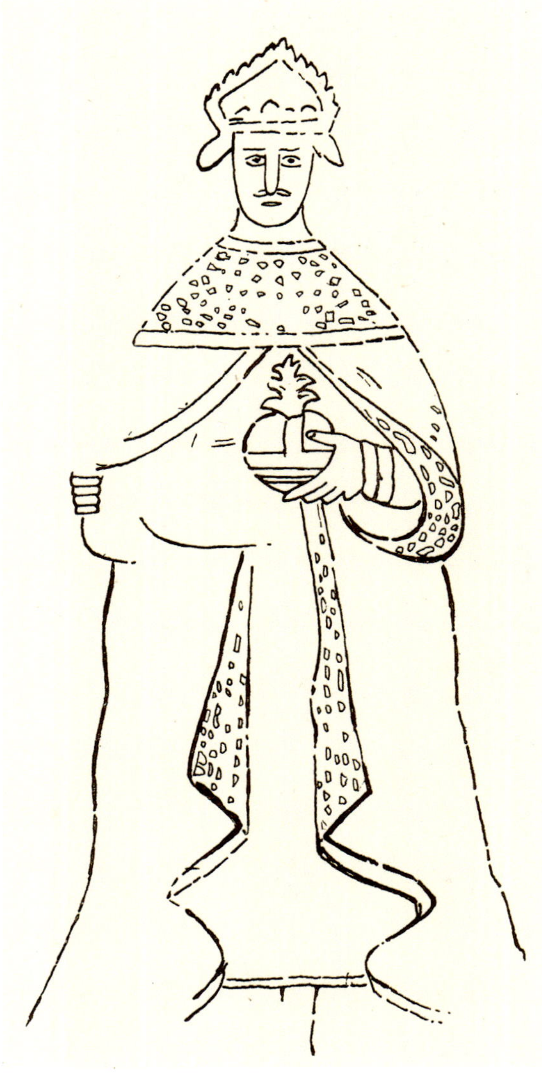

Breage. Henry VI. (Plate 7, *JRIC*, XIV, 1901)

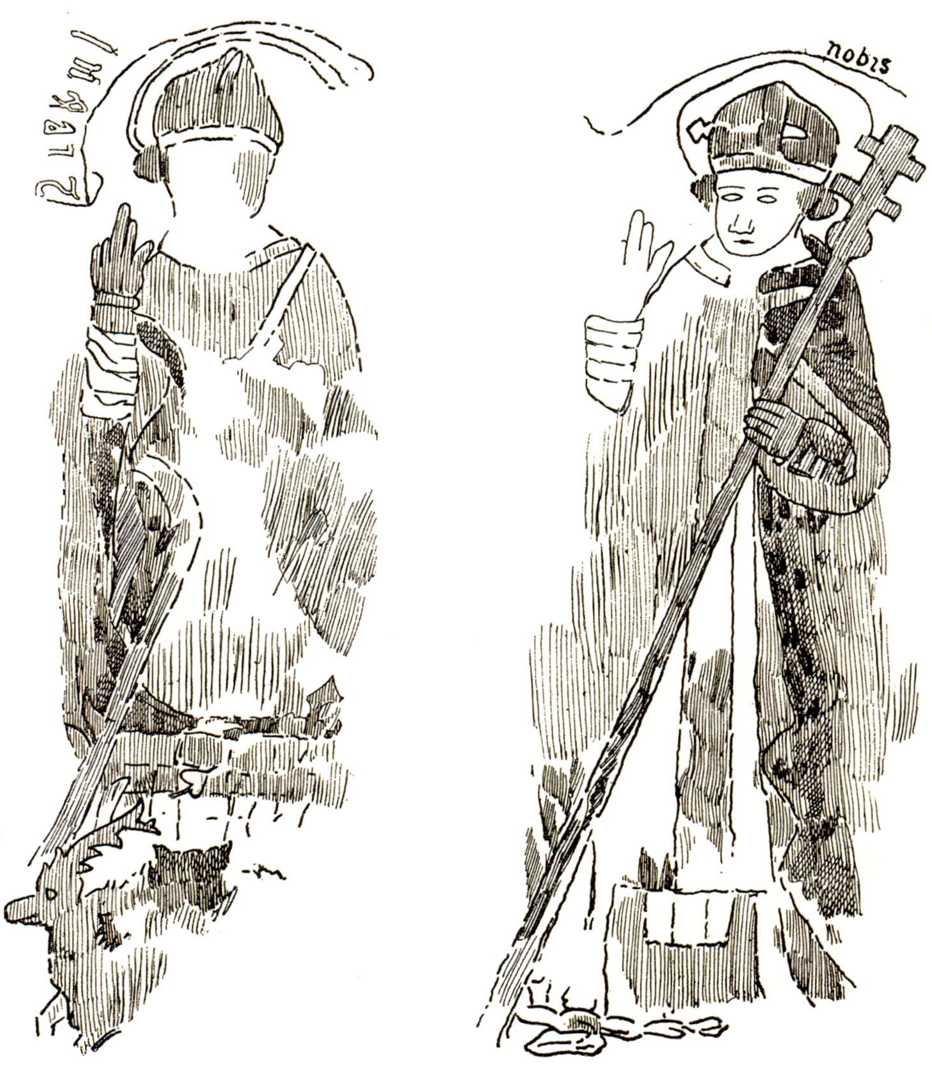

Above left and above right: Breage. Giles with deer and Thomas Becket with dagger through mitre. (Plates 8–9, *JRIC*, XIV, 1901)

Canterbury, too. At St Michael's Mount, pilgrims could see the sword and spurs of this most unwarlike of English kings, whose canonisation was thwarted due to Henry VIII's matrimonial difficulties.

Giles' scroll reads 'St Aegid' and the mitred saint raises his right hand in blessing while a deer is attacked by a beast at his feet. The Provence shrine of St Giles was on the pilgrim routes to Compostela and the Holy Land and at least 162 English churches were dedicated to him. To the east, Thomas Becket is shown as archbishop of Canterbury with a dagger through his mitre. He was joint patron of St Buryan and Glasney College, Penryn, and sole patron of Bodmin's churchyard chapel.

Local saints occur on walls elsewhere, with a thirteenth-century probable image of Morwenna on the north wall of Morwenstow chancel. Shown with veil, yellow robe and cloak, blessing a kneeling priest with her right hand, she holds a book in her left. Morwenna was a daughter of Brychan and in 1478 was described as a virgin saint buried in the church.

Neot and Gueriir may be the kneeling, red-gowned saints in an early fourteenth-century painting on the back wall of the Easter Sepulchre or saints' tomb at St Neot (see p. 29). The figures kneel before Christ, Saviour of the World, with an orb at his feet like the Zennor Christ (p. 37). At St Neot three coiling black ropes on each side link haloed saints to heads with spotted wings – perhaps souls – and there is a worn inscription below.

An image of St Crida, local patron of Creed, was found in a window splay of Lanivet's north aisle in 1864. The painting showed a crowned woman with a sceptre, with other

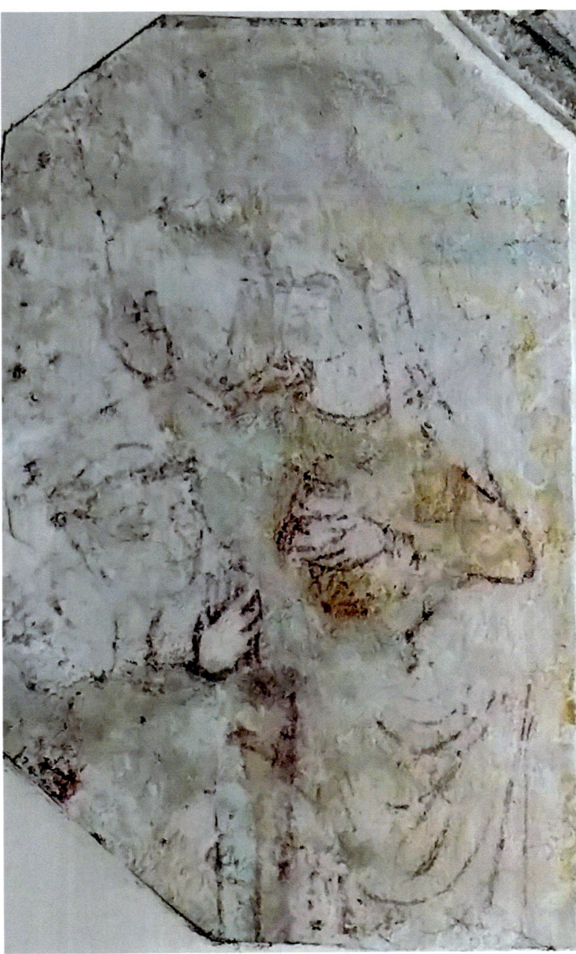

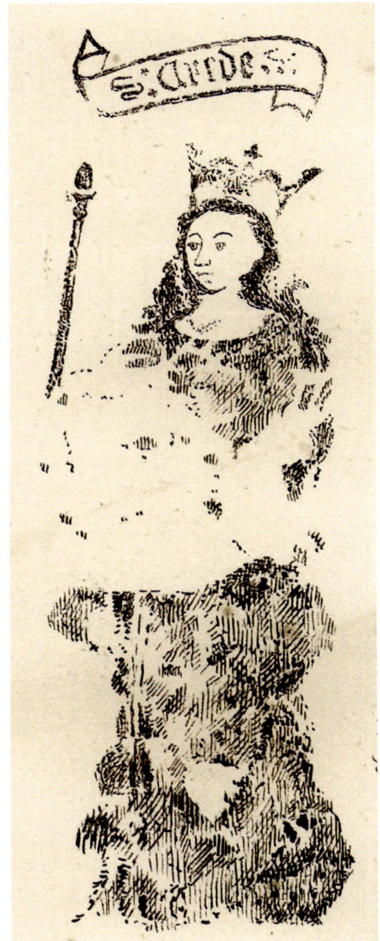

Above left: Morwenstow. Morwenna, thirteenth century.

Above right: Lanivet. Crida, fifteenth century. (Illustration by William Iago; plate 3, *JRIC*, I, 1870)

paintings on the south side; all now lost. Land belonging to Lanivet church called Creedos Park in Padstow parish may mark a chapel site. At Landulph in 1559 two paintings showed Dilic (Dyllytt) and Leonard, then joint patrons of the church. These were destroyed as objects of veneration so may have been panels, not wall paintings. Local girls were christened Dilecta in 1543 and 1573, a pet form of Dilic, a daughter of King Brychan.

St Petroc was probably among the most painted of local saints. In 1512–14, painter William Potter received 18*s* 8*d* 'for the painting of Seynte Petrok' in the newly completed Holy Rood chapel at the Berry, Bodmin. Just under a third of the cost was raised from the gifts of Elizabeth Fykke, priest Thomas Hayly, John Vyan and weaver John Wyll, who gave 12*d*, two sums of 4*d*, and a bullock worth 4*s*, respectively. Could the fragmentary painting of a bishop in Constantine church also represent Petroc?

At Cubert church in the seventeenth century there was a depiction of St Cuthbert as bishop wearing a mitre and holding a crosier. Although the painting probably represented the northern saint, Cubert is the location of the famous Holywell. Only accessible for about an hour at low tide, cures involved passing sick children through a cleft inside the cave on Ascension Day. In medieval times there was a chapel and well at Trevornick halfway between church and cave where people waited for the tide to turn. The name Cubert was certainly a parish Christian name.

A lost wall painting of Christopher with local resonance was recorded but not saved at Ludgvan. Also showing Reynard the fox being tried and hanged, this painting may have advertised the power of Ludewan's holy well, Ludgvan folk believing that if baptised in its water they would never be hanged.

The moralistic Warning to Sabbath Breakers or St Sunday paintings also have local relevance. One was drawn before being lost at Lanivet, others survive at Breage, St Just-in-Penwith and Poundstock; with a fifth depicted in glass at St Neot. Four similar wall paintings are known from Wales, three from Buckinghamshire, two each for Suffolk,

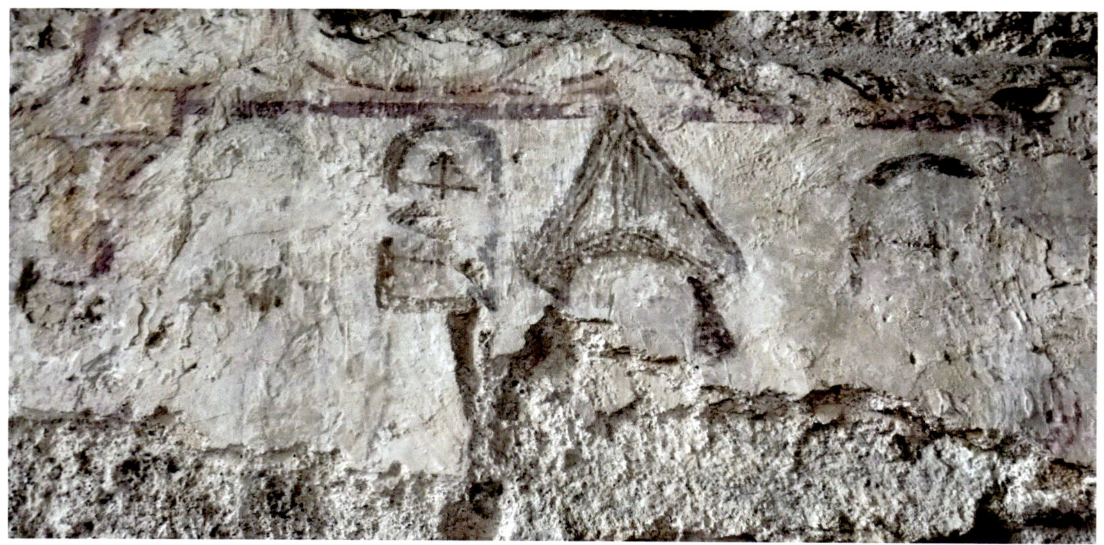

Constantine. Bishop, possibly Petroc, with chapel behind, medieval.

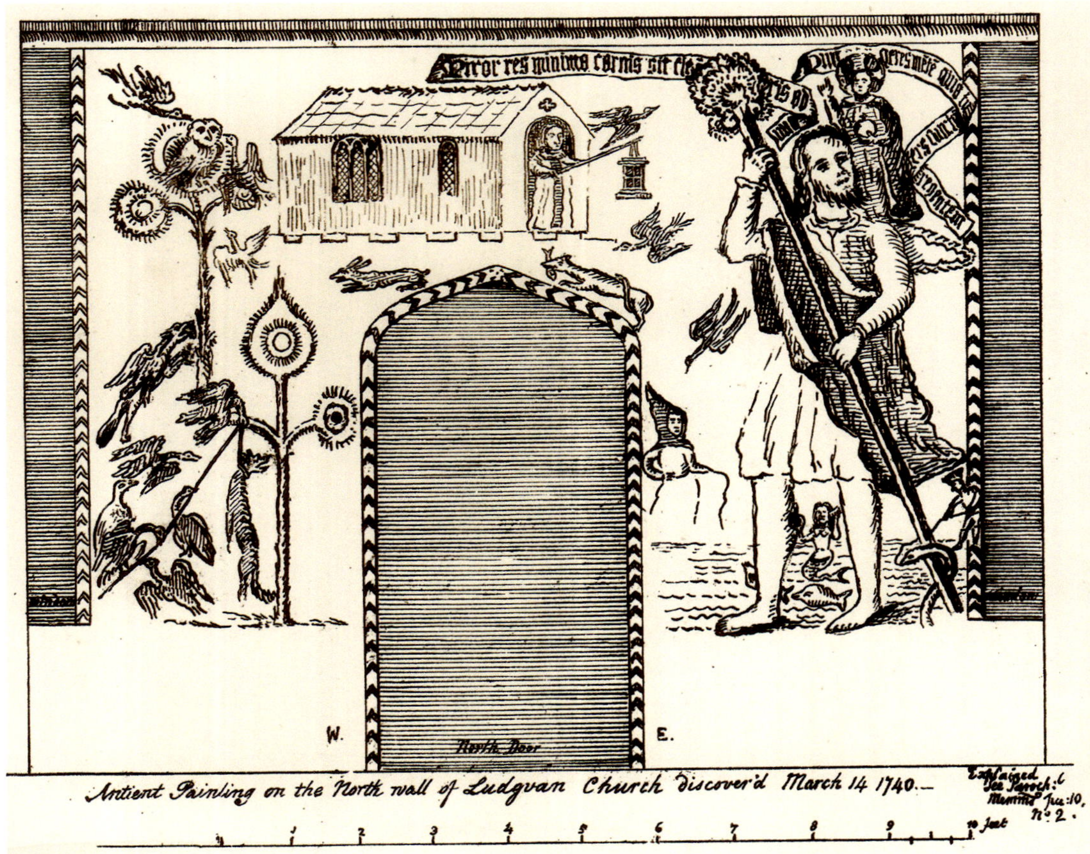

Ludgvan. St Christopher and Reynard the Fox, early sixteenth century. (William Iago copy of 1740 illustration by William Borlase, *JRIC*, IV, 1872, opp., p. 50)

Sussex and Wilshire, while Berkshire, Cambridgeshire, Essex, Gloucestershire, Hampshire and Herefordshire have one a-piece. The European concentration of such images is in Italy and the Alps, with an outlier in the Czech Republic.

Trade tools that inflict wounds on Christ if used on a Sunday were wood-cut based, but between Christ's legs at Breage there is a lute and higher up a harp. This was a clear warning to the wealthy Godolphin family not to play music on Sundays. Other items relate to the local fishing industry include a fishhook embedded in Christ's right leg, a reel above the lute, an anchor to the left and at St Just a fish in a boat. A tinner's poll pick once appeared in glass at St Neot, and at Breage a medieval tin ingot, partly obscured by green paint above the anchor, is a good match for the St Mawes ingot now in the Cornwall Museum and Art Gallery.

Wall paintings with religious subjects could also be found in domestic settings like Cullacott in Werrington parish, now owned by the Landmark Trust. Unable to afford tapestry, the Colecotes chose a good painter and a fictive tapestry was painted *c.* 1525 behind the dais in the open hall. The tapestry is drawn back to reveal a crowned Virgin

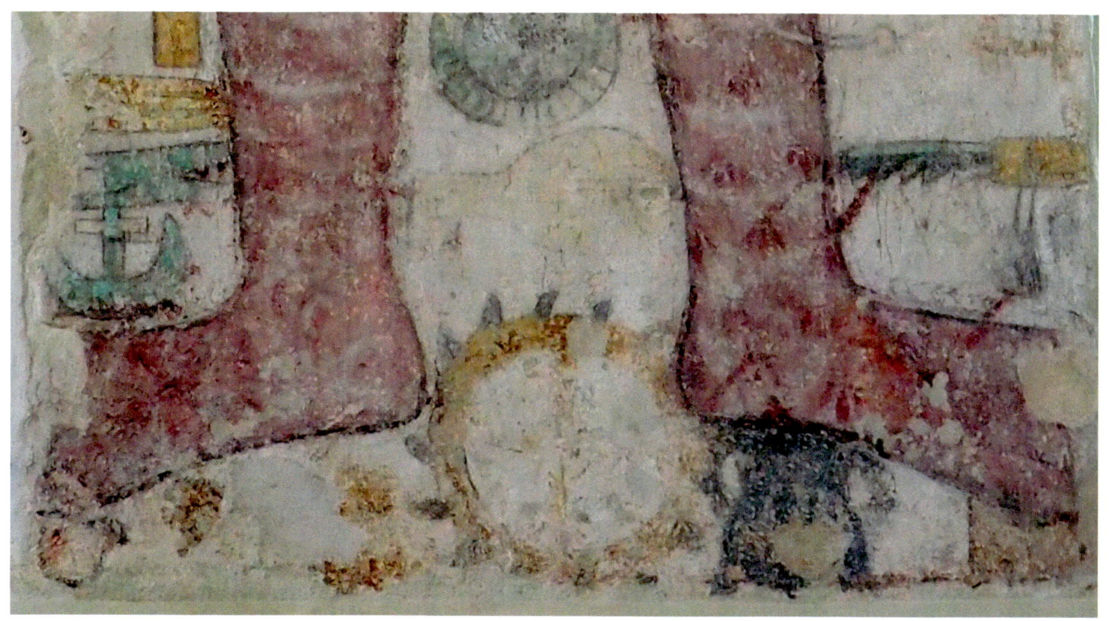

Breage. Detail of anchor, tin ingot, and very faded lute in middle from Warning to Sabbath Breakers (St Sunday), late fifteenth century. (Photo by Nina Hocking)

and Child in a mandorla over the high table, with kneeling donor figures, not angels. In 1505–06 a similar Assumption of the Virgin painting in Bodmin church cost over 20*s* to paint comparable to the cost of a stained glass window. A dancing figure on the wall to the left at Cullacott is supposed to be St James the Great, while a St George occupies a private first-floor chamber at the other end of the hall.

Christ had more painted images than anyone else, including St Sunday and St Saviour images. In 1493–94, a Corpus Christi painting in the north aisle of Bodmin church cost over 26*s*. An under-drawing of Christ in his tomb being censed by angels at Lanteglos-by-Fowey is particularly fine and there was a similar image in the votive chapel in Cotehele woods. Lost crucifixions are noted at St Clement and Talland, with a former harrowing of hell, showing Christ bringing the dead from the underworld, at Lanivet. Christ as the man of sorrows was once at Lanivet and survives at Linkinhorne combined with the seven works of mercy.

Mary could appear in many guises in wall paintings, as in other mediums. In the south aisle at Lanivet she was once the Virgin of Mercy, sheltering souls under her cloak. Surprisingly, in view of her survival in other mediums, there are only three Marian fragments now, at Cullacott, Breage and Poundstock (a Virgin of Mercy), while her rosary beads appear on the south wall at Linkinhorne. At Gulval, Mary's Annunciation lily pot is painted on the west face of an octagonal pillar by the rood loft.

Paintings of St Christopher were to be found in every church. In 1512–14, 2*s* 4*d* was paid to the painter John Hoyge for 'the newe payntynge of Seynte Christofor' at the Holy Rood chapel at Berry, Bodmin, probably a touching-up of an existing one. There are lost paintings at St Clement, Ludgvan, Mylor, Talland and Virginstow and survivals at Breage,

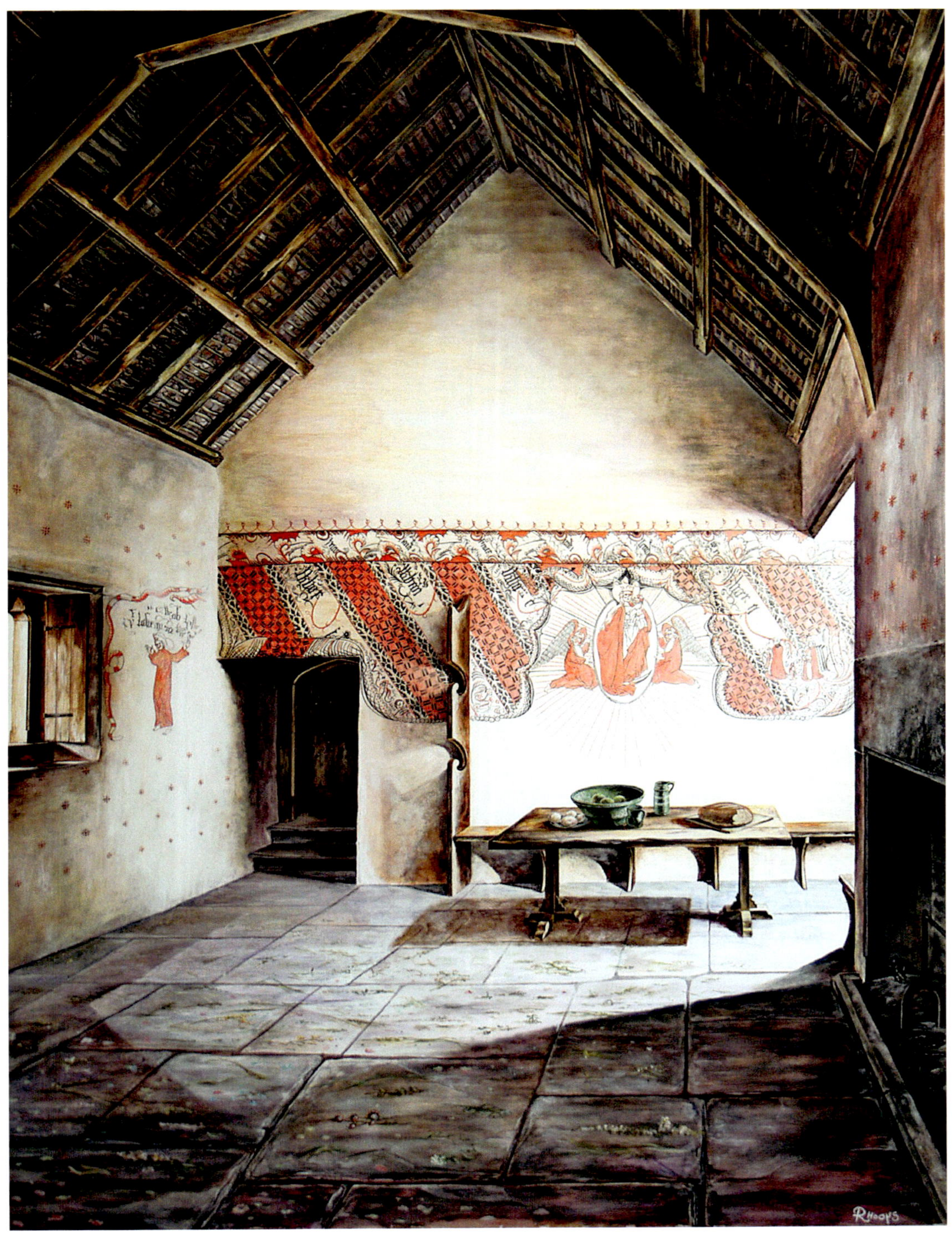

Cullacott. Reconstruction of hall painting, *c.* 1520s. (Rhoops Ford for Keystone Historic Buildings Consultants)

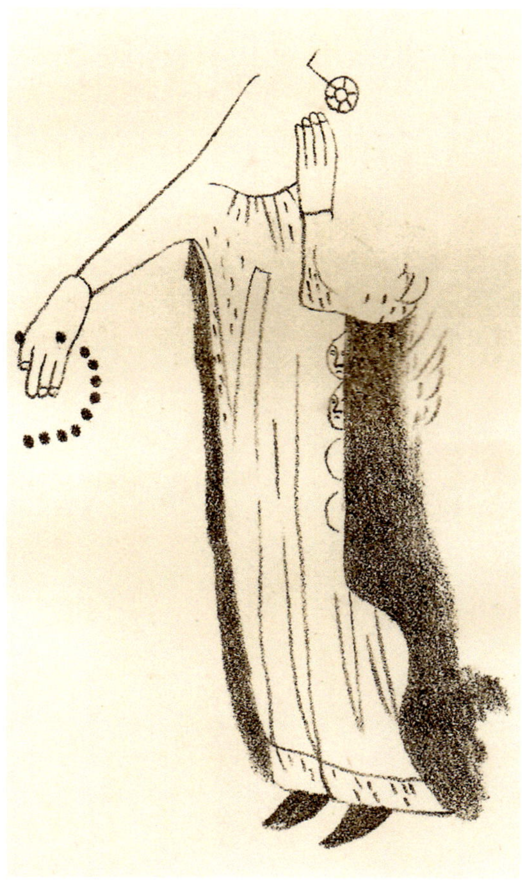

Lanivet. Virgin of Mercy, fifteenth
century. (T.Q. Couch, *Parochialia –
Lanivet*, *JRIC*, IV, 1865, pp. 71–82; plate ii)

St Keverne and Poughill twice, the southern being probably paid for by St Christopher
and St Apollonia's guild. Such paintings derived from fifteenth-century woodcuts, apart
from Mylor, with a mermaid occuring at Breage, Poughill and formerly Ludgvan.

St George appears four times with dragon, including doubled-up versions above
the south arcade at Calstock, St Just-in-Penwith and Cullacott where the horse wears
chainmail. The Archangel St Michael fights the dragon at Breage, and formerly weighed
souls at Poundstock and probably Linkinhorne. Other single figures include a lost Andrew
at Stratton, and Roche locked away with his plague sores, angel and dog on the north
side of the Lady Chapel at Launceston St Thomas. At Mylor, fourteenth-century saints
were decapitated when the nave wall was lowered in the late medieval period to create a
uniform-height church.

Rood Loft Dadoes

There are only five painted dadoes in Cornwall today, at Budock, Gunwalloe, Lanreath,
Mawnan and Poundstock. Fifty-five painted panels survive, which is fewer than in the
single Devon church of Wolborough. Many Cornish rood lofts were still being created
in the run-up to the Reformation, and had carved rather than painted bases. Only at

Budock and Lanreath are painted dadoes still *in situ*, with many panels scraped at the latter. Carved dadoes were painted: red, green, ochre and black at St Buryan, red, blue and yellow at Madron, and a more naturalistic palette at Sancreed.

No image of a local saint has been identified among the scanty Cornish survivals but at East Portlemouth in Devon a probable Winwaloe holds a church, and Sidwell appears on many Devon screens including Hennock, holding a scythe and spare head. Apostles dominate, as in Devon, but in Cornwall have moustache-less beards. In the nave at Budock, red-cloaked apostles alternate with green-cloaked prophets, with the first four apostles at Mawnan and eight extant at Gunwalloe. Philip, Bartholomew and Jude represent the end of a run of apostles at Poundstock. There is space enough for apostles in the nave at Lanreath.

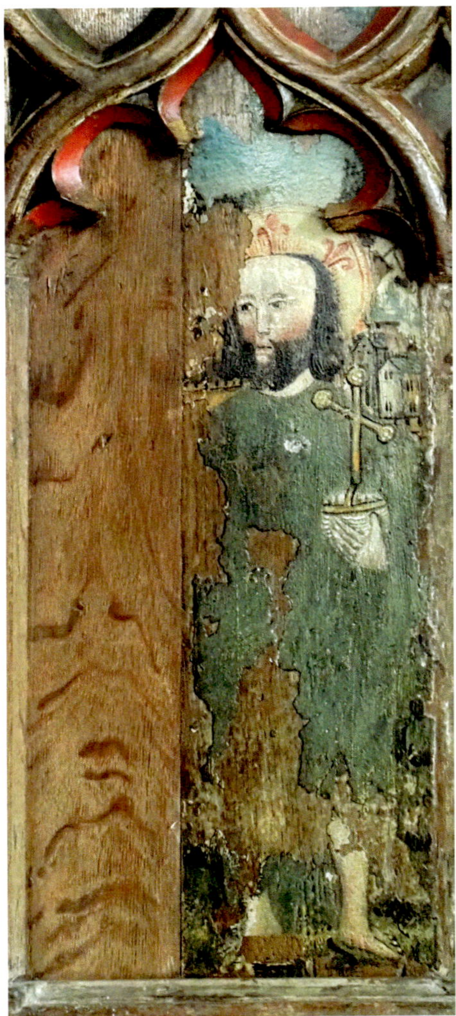

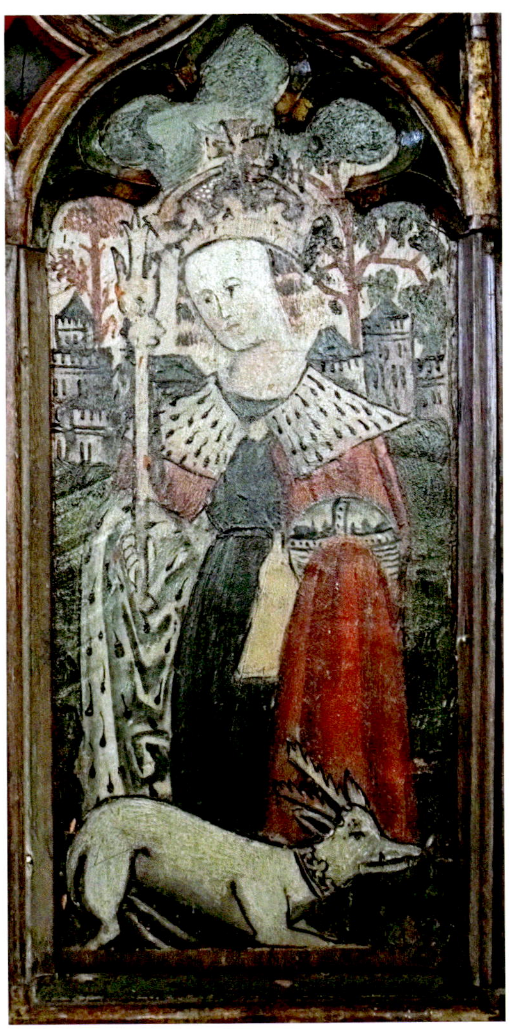

Above left: Lanreath. Christ as Saviour, *c.* 1520. (Photo by Eric Berry)

Above right: Lanreath. Henry VI, *c.* 1520. (Photo by Eric Berry)

At Lanreath the early sixteenth-century dado paintings are of exceptional quality (despite restoration), and panels include idealised landscape backgrounds like the Cotehele stained glass. Subjects include Christ as Saviour in green holding an orb with bare legs and space for a St Mary Magdalene, and Henry VI, with sceptre, wearing an ermine-collared red cloak over a green robe with his white hart at his feet. A south-aisle door panel shows the Visitation, suggesting a missing Annunciation on the chancel doors. St Ursula holds an arrow on another south door panel. Then come eight smaller, more restored figures of the four doctors of the church and popular female saints Apollonia, Sitha, Dorothy and Barbara.

At Poundstock, male and female saints start with Blaise with his wool comb. A fully erased saint follows (possibly Thomas Becket), and then come Sitha, John the Baptist and Apollonia with tooth clamped in a pair of oversize pliers. Apollonia, Barbara and possibly Dorothy occurred at Budock among seven maidens, with flowers in their hair in the north aisle.

All images of wood or stone would once have been painted, and a few stone statues, like the alabaster of St Christopher at St Ive, retain some paint. Fragments of brightly painted alabaster reredoses still exist at Lanteglos-by-Fowey, Lostwithiel and Mabe.

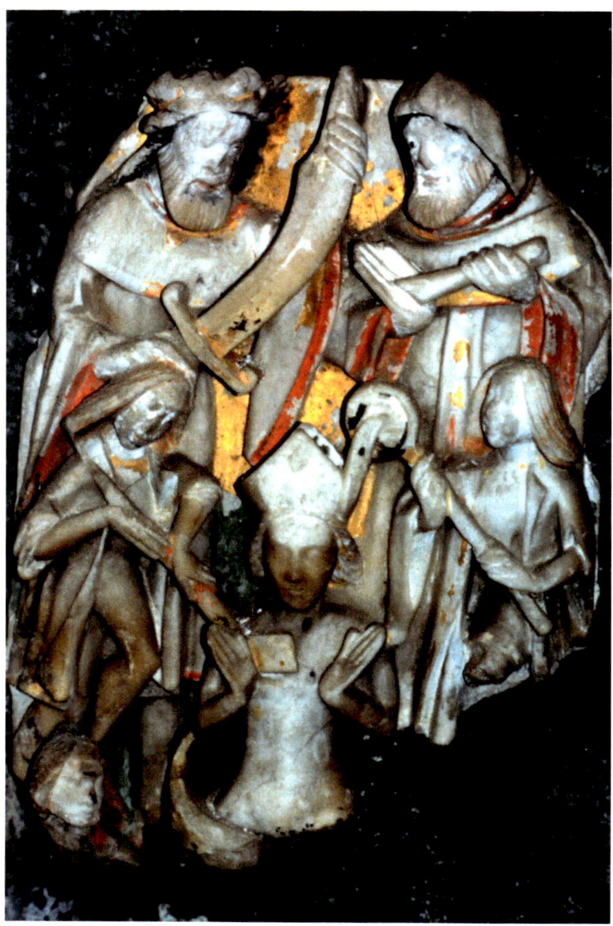

Mabe. St John the Evangelist alabaster panel, fifteenth century.

Epilogue

In 1537, John Carpyssacke ordered a painted banner for St Keverne, a place known for rebellion since 1497. Unfortunately, the painter he approached worked for William Godolphin, a government agent. Carpyssacke was probably executed at Helston town end as a result. The banner should have depicted a Resurrected Christ holding a banner, Mary holding her breast in her hands and John the Baptist (similar groupings occur in Doom paintings where Mary's role was to intercede with Christ). On the other side of the banner, the king and queen (Henry VIII and Jane Seymour) were to be represented with people kneeling and petitioning the picture of Christ that the king would let them have their saints' days again. Carpyssacke's banner was a visual response to the northern rebellion known as the Pilgrimage of Grace and the Act of Parliament of 1536, which severely reduced the number of saints' days.

Also in 1537, Simon Heynes, the Protestant dean of Exeter, arrived in Cornwall, hammer in hand, to challenge the Catholic Arundells in their heartland at Mawgan in Pydar. In 1538, St Thomas Becket was erased from screens and prayer books and candles only allowed before the rood and Easter Sepulchre. After a partial amnesty under Queen

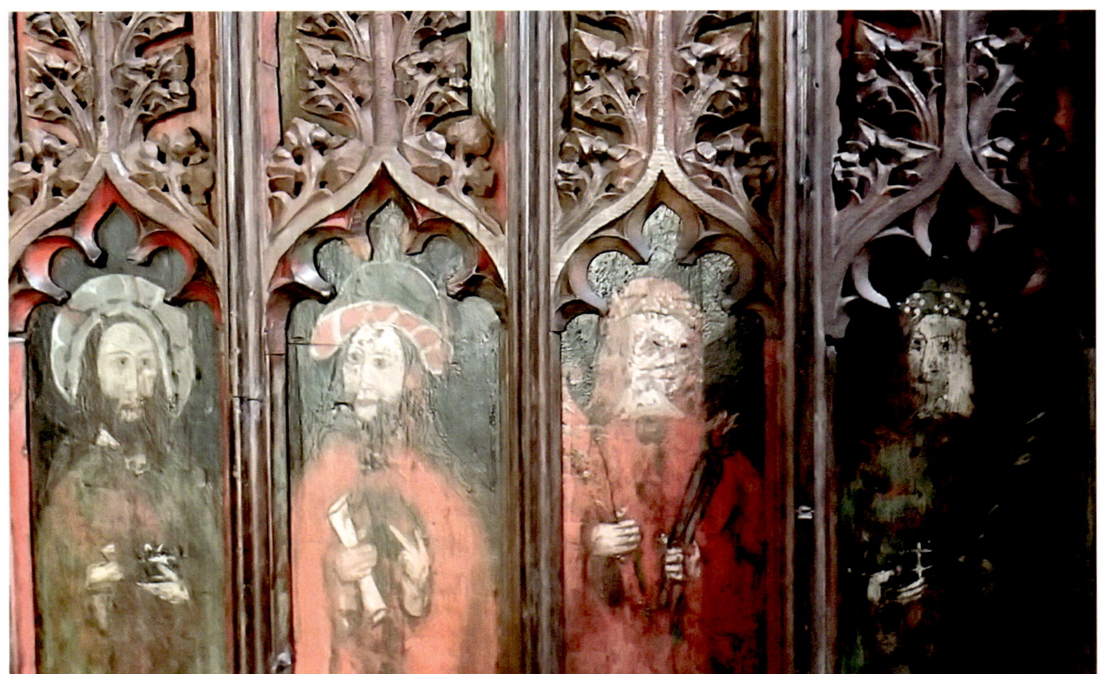

Budock. St Andrew, prophet, St Apollonia, female martyr, fifteenth century.

Mary (1553–58), during which Stratton parish had a new St Andrew painted, most local saints were doomed.

The major period of iconoclasm for Cornwall seems to have been *c.* 1650–61 at the end of the Civil War, led by Parliamentarian soldiers as we saw in the introduction. Zennor's west tower Christ was singled out for annihilation in its niche, probably by Major Peter Ceely's men from their nearby base at St Ives. Other stone international saints lost their heads or were defaced with hammers; even John the Baptist's camel lost an eye at St Kew (see p. 53).

Only apostles and prophets were exempt, as can clearly be seen on the rood loft dado at Budock. Budock, like Zennor, was particularly vulnerable as soldiers were stationed at Pendennis Castle in the parish. All Budock's female saints had their eyes scratched out, but the likely perpetrators, Colonel Charles Shrubsall's men, pierced holes through the eyes of Apollonia and another female martyr in a deliberate act of blind hatred.

As the multitude of empty statue niches show, iconoclasm and image breaking was universal, and visual survival rare even in Catholic Cornwall. With local and Brittonic saints depicted as bishops, hermits, kings, queens or martyrs, like their international or Saxon rivals, they should have been equally targeted. Yet of all the extant local and Brittonic saints' carved images, only at St Erme is there a hammer-broken nose, beard and hair loss. This is in contrast to many defaced and broken international saints and half the Saxon and Norse saints' images. Where local saints were combined with international ones, as on lantern crosses, they were rendered unrecognisable, but fared better when part of church fabric. Arguably such worn and cherished visualisations of Cornwall's saints helped to keep their stories alive. Go out and look for yourself – there is more to find.

Places to Visit

The locations below offer a chance to see possible local or Brittonic saints' images, their symbols and relics as well as Saxon, Norse and international saints. Some images remain speculative and numbers in brackets indicate chapters where more information can be found. For most lantern cross images, see Andrew Langdon and Ann Preston-Jones, Ann, *Illuminating our Lantern Crosses* (Truro, 2022). CMAG = Cornwall Museum and Art Gallery + = unique Cornish saint including made-up ones.

Cornish and Brittonic Saints

St Austell	Austell, Mewan (3).
Bodmin	Petroc's casket (2).
Breage	Corentin (6).
Constantine	Constantine (3), Petroc? (6).
St Erme	Erme+ (3).
Germoe	Germoc+ (1).
Gwinear	Gwinear's stag+ (2).
St Issey	Children of Brychan[*], Nectan, Petroc (3).
Kenwyn	Kenwyn (3).
St Keverne	Keverne (3).
Ladock	Ladoc+? (3).
Lamorran	Moren+? (5).
Lanlivery	Brivet+ (3).
St Levan	Salamon's fish (4).
Little Petherick	Petroc's horn, sword and bell (2/4).
Ludgvan	Ludewan+ (1/3).
Mawgan in Meneage	Maugan (3).
Mawgan in Pydar	Maugan lantern cross bishop (3).
Mawnan	Mawnan+? (3).
Morwenstow	Morwenna+ (6).
St Neot	Neot's fish (4); Clair, Lallu+, Mabyn, Manac+, Meubred+, Neot, Petroc (5), Gueriir and Neot (6).
St Newlyn East	Newlyn+ (3-4).
Padstow	Petroc (3).
Probus	Probus'+ skull? (2).

---

* The Children of Brychan included twelve female saints – Dilic, Endelient, Issey, Juliana, Mabyn, Menfre, Merewenna, Morwenna, Tetha, Wencu, Wenna and Wensent – plus Adwen, Cleder, Keri, Nectan and Wenheden, and seven other mainly Welsh male saints.

St Sampson Golant	Samson (4).
Sithney	Sithney (3).
St Winnow	Winnoc (5).
Victoria and Albert Museum	Endelient+ (4).

For early twentieth-century images see especially St Hilary and Truro Cathedral choir stalls.

Saxon and Norse Saints

Braddock	Sidwell (4).
Laneast	Sidwell (4), Etheldreda (5).
Poughill	Olaf's crown and crossed battle axe(s) (4).
St Winnow	Sidwell (5).

Alphabetical list of international saints's images including fragments but not symbols

All Saints	St Neot (5).
Ambrose	St Kew (5); Lanreath (6).
Andrew	St Austell, St Dominick, St Merryn, Padstow, South Hill (3); Cotehele, St Ives, St Sampson Golant (4); Lanteglos-by-Camelford, St Neot (5); Budock, Gunwalloe, Mawnan (6).
Anne	Mabe (3); Cotehele (5).
Anthony	Tresillian (3); Cotehele (4); St Sampson Golant (5).
Apollonia	Budock, Lanreath, Poundstock (6).
Augustine	St Kew (5); Breage, Lanreath (6).
Barbara	St Neot (5); Budock, Lanreath (6).
Bartholomew	St Austell, St Dominick, Lostwithiel, St Merryn, Padstow, South Hill (3); Braddock, St Sampson Golant (4); Lanteglos-by-Camelford (5); Budock (6).
Blaise	Poundstock (6).
Christopher	St Ive (3); Lanteglos-by-Camelford, St Neot, St Winnow (5); Breage, St Keverne, Poughill (6).
Clement	Withiel (3).
Dennis	St Dennis (3).
Dorothy	Budock?, Lanreath (6).
Elizabeth	Lanreath (6).
Erasmus	Cotehele (4).
Francis	Cotehele (4).
Gabriel	Madron (4); Cotehele, Lanteglos-by-Fowey, St Neot, Quethiock, Sithney (5).
George	Launceston St Mary Magdalene (3); St Neot, St Winnow (5); Calstock, Cullacott, St Just-in-Penwith (6).
German	St Neot (5).

Gregory	St Neot (5); Lanreath (6).
Giles	Breage (6).
Helen	St Ewe (4); St Neot (5).
Henry VI	Breage, Lanreath (6).
Hilary	Breage (6).
James the Great	St Austell, St Breward (old school); St Dominick, St Merryn, Padstow, Perranuthnoe, South Hill (3); St Levan (4); Lanteglos-by-Camelford, St Neot, St Sampson Golant (5); Budock, Cullacott in Werrington?, Gunwalloe, Mawnan (6).
James the Less	St Austell, St Dominick, St Merryn, Padstow, South Hill (3); St Austell, Cotehele (4); Gunwalloe (6).
Jerome	Lanreath (6).
Jesus	St Austell, Duloe, Lostwithiel, Mabe, Mullion, North Tamerton, Zennor (3); Cotehele, Ludgvan now CMAG, Morval, St Sampson Golant, Tregaminion and Tywardreath (4); Cotehele, St Kew, Laneast, St Neot, St Winnow (5); Breage, St Just-in-Penwith, Lanreath, Linkinhorne, Poundstock (6) and see Christopher, Mary, Trinity.
John	St Austell, St Dominick, Gulval, Mabe, St Mabyn, St Merryn, Padstow, South Hill (3); Antony, St Austell, Cotehele (4); Altarnun, St Neot, St Winnow (5); Budock, Gunwalloe, Mawnan (6) and see Jesus.
John the Baptist	St Kew (3); Antony, Cotehele (4); St Neot (5).
Jude	St Austell, St Dominick, St Merryn, Padstow, South Hill (3); Cotehele (4); Budock, Gunwalloe, Poundstock (6).
Katherine	Cotehele, St Kew, St Neot (5); Lanreath(6).
Lawrence	Lanteglos-by-Fowey (3); St Sampson Golant, Tywardreath (4); St Kew (5).
Leonard	St Neot, St Winnow (5).
Luke	Gulval, St Mabyn (3); Antony (4); St Neot (5).
Margaret	CMAG (4); St Neot (5).
Mark	Gulval, St Mabyn (3); Antony (4); St Neot (5).
Martin	Launceston St Mary Magdalene (3).
Mary	St Allen, Botus Fleming, St Austell, St Issey, Launceston St Mary Magdalene, Sennen, Talland (3); Cardinham, Davidstow, St Keverne Madron, (4); Breage,St Breock, Cotehele, St Enoder, St Kew, Lanteglos-by-Fowey, Mullion, St Neot, Quethiock, Sheviock, Sithney, St Winnow (5); Breage, Cullacott in Werrington, Lanreath (6) and see Anne, Jesus.
Mary Magdalene	Launceston St Mary Magdalene (3); Budock (6).
Mary Salome	CMAG (5).

Matthew	St Austell, St Dominick, Gulval, St Mabyn, St Merryn, Padstow, South Hill (3); Antony (4); St Neot (5); Budock, Gunwalloe (6).
Matthias	St Austell, St Dominick, St Merryn, Padstow, South Hill (3); Cotehele, St Sampson Golant (4); St Neot (5); Budock, (6).
Michael	St Austell, Cotehele, St Ives (4); St Kew, St Winnow (5); Breage, Linkinhorne, Poundstock (6).
Nicholas	St Germans? (4).
Paul	Cotehele (4); St Neot (5).
Peter	St Austell, St Cleer, St Dominick, St Merryn, Padstow, South Hill (3); Braddock, Cotehele, St Ives, Luxulyan (4); Lanteglos-by-Camelford, St Neot (5); Gunwalloe, Mawnan (6).
Philip	St Austell, St Dominick, St Merryn, Padstow, South Hill (3); Cotehele (4); Lanteglos-by-Camelford (5); Budock, Poundstock (6).
Roche	Cotehele (4); Launceston St Thomas (6).
Sebastian	Cotehele (4).
Simon	St Austell, St Dominick, St Merryn, Padstow, South Hill (3); Cotehele (4); Budock, Gunwalloe (6).
Sitha	Lanreath, Poundstock (6).
Stephen	Mabe (3); St Neot (5).
Thomas	St Austell, St Dominick, St Merryn, Padstow, South Hill (3); Cotehele, St Sampson Golant (4); Budock (6).
Thomas Becket	Breage (6).
Trinity	St Austell, St Gluvias, Sithney (3); Egloskerry (5).
Ursula	Lanreath (6).

Bibliography

Beacham, Peter and Pevsner, Nikolaus, *Cornwall* (New Haven and London: Yale University Press, 2014).

Cheetham, Francis, *Alabaster Images of Medieval England* (Woodbridge, Suffolk: The Boydell Press, 2003).

Coate, Mary, *Cornwall in the Great Civil War and Interregnum 1642-1660* (Truro: D. Bradford Barton Ltd, 2nd edn, 1963), pp. 333–4 for Joseph Maye.

Coomber, Jane E., 'Medieval Painting in Cornwall', May 1980', MA thesis (Royal Institution of Cornwall).

Doble, G. H., "Cornish Saints Series" (Long Compton: The "King's Stone" Press, 1923–41).

Enys, J. D., Peter, Thurstan C. & Whitley, H. Michell, 'Mural Paintings in Cornish Churches', *Journal of the Royal Institution of Cornwall* (1901), pp. 136–60, 13 plates.

Gentle, Nicola Jane, 'Three Late Fifteenth-Early Sixteenth-Century Chapel Furnishings Belonging to the Edgcumbe Family in Cornwall', *The Antiquaries Journal* (2024), pp. 145–68.

Graham-Dixon, Andrew, *A History of British Art* (London: BBC Books, 1996, chapter one 'Dreams and Hammers', pp. 12-45).

Gray, Todd, *A Gazeteer of Ancient Bench Ends in Cornwall's Parish Churches* (Exeter: The Mint Press, 2016).

John, Catherine Rachel, *The Saints of Cornwall* (Redruth, 1981).

Langdon, Andrew G. & Preston-Jones, Ann, *Illuminating our Lantern Crosses* (Truro, 2022).

Mattingly, Joanna, 'Stories in the Glass – Reconstructing the St Neot Pre-Reformation Glazing Scheme', *Journal of the Royal Institution of Cornwall* (2000), pp. 9–55.

Mattingly, Joanna, 'Pre-Reformation saints' cults in Cornwall, with particular reference to the St Neot windows' in *Celtic Hagiography and Saints' Cults*, ed. Jane Cartwright (Cardiff: University of Wales Press, 2003), pp. 249–70.

Mattingly, Joanna (ed.), *Stratton Churchwardens' Accounts 1512–1578* (Woodbridge, Suffolk: Devon and Cornwall Record Society and The Boydell Press, 2018).

Mattingly, Joanna, *Churches of Cornwall* (Stroud: Amberley Publishing, 2023).

Mattingly, Joanna, 'Rood Loft Construction, Decoration, and Cult Focus in Ashburton (Devon) and Cornwall from the 1450s to 1548' in *Education and Religion in Medieval and Renaissance England: Essays in Honour of Nicholas Orme*, ed. Jonathan Barry, James G. Clark and William Richardson (Donington: Shaun Tyas, 2023), pp. 74–110.

Mattingly, Joanna with Shapland, John, 'Report on Documentary Sources for the Berry Tower (Holy Rood Chapel) Bodmin' in *Archaeological Report, Watching Brief, Excavations & Historical Record at Berry Tower Bodmin 23rd August 2005*, ed. Rhoops Ford (Truro: Scott and Company, 2005), pp. 7–84.

Marks, Richard, *Image and Devotion in Late Medieval England* (Stroud: Sutton Publishing, 2004).

Olson, L., *Early Monasteries in Cornwall* (Woodbridge, Suffolk: The Boydell Press, 1989).

Orme, Nicholas (ed.), *Nicholas Roscarrock's Lives of the Saints: Cornwall and Devon* (Exeter: Devon and Cornwall Record Society, 1992).

Orme, Nicholas, *The Saints of Cornwall* (Oxford: Oxford University Press, 2000).

Orme, Nicholas, *Going to Church in Medieval England* (New Haven and London: Yale University Press, 2021).

Padel, Oliver, 'Local Saints and Place-Names in Cornwall' in *Local Saints and Local Churches*, ed. Alan Thacker and Richard Sharpe (Oxford: Oxford University Press, 2002), pp. 303–60.

Preston-Jones, Ann, Langdon, Andrew and Elizabeth Okasha, *Ancient and High Crosses of Cornwall – Cornwall's Earliest, Tallest and Finest Medieval Stone Crosses* (Exeter: University of Exeter Press, 2021).

Reiss, Athene, *The Sunday Christ – Sabbatarianism in English medieval wall painting* (Oxford: British Archaeological Report, 2000).

Rose-Troup, Frances, *The Western Rebellion of 1549* (London: Smith, Elder & Co., 1913).

Whiting, Robert, 'Abominable Idols: Images and Image-Breaking under Henry VIII', *Journal of Ecclesiastical History*, vol. 33 (1982), pp. 30–47.

Wilks, Diane, *A Cloud of Witnesses – Medieval Panel Paintings of Saints in Devon Churches* (Broadclyst, Exeter: Azure Publications, 1988).

Wilks, Diane, *A Cloud of Witnesses – Showing the Path to Heaven – A Celebration of Painted Panel in Devon Churches* (Broadclyst, Exeter: Azure Publications, 2014)

Wilson, Helen, *From 'Lady' Woodcarvers to Professionals – The Remarkable Pinwill Sisters* (Plymouth: Willow Productions, 2021).

Woodcock, Alex, 'Atlantic Gothic: the Architectural Sculpture of the "Master of St Endellion"' in *What is unique about Cornish buildings? Proceedings of the 2019 CBG conference*, ed. Paul Holden (Donnington: Shaun Tyas, 2023), pp. 78–95.

For stained glass, see Michael Swift Archives (www.visitstainedglass.uk) and *Corpus Vitrearum Medii Aevi – Medieval Stained Glass in Britain* (www.cvma.ac.uk).

Acknowledgements

Thanks to David Mattingly and Graeme Kirkham for initial editing; and Paul Cockerham, Andrew Langdon, Oliver Padel, Ann Preston-Jones and Michael Swift for reading and commenting on specific chapters. All shared ideas with me and Ann and Andrew supplied many photographs. Mark Charter, Eric Berry, Nina Hocking, Piers Kent and Alan Stout took photographs especially for this book. Nick Grant and Jenny Bennett at Amberley Publishing have also been unfailingly helpful. Many others made contributions including Jo Cox, Christine Edwards, Nicola Gentle, Miriam Gill, James Gossip, John Gould, Charles and Diana Hall, Isobel Harvey, Rachel Hunt, Helena Nightingale, Jacky Nowakowski, Nicholas Orme, Pat Penhallurick, Heather Stout, Moira Tangye, John Thorp, Julia Whiteside and Helen Wilson. I am also grateful to churchwardens and vicars who opened churches especially for me and to parishioners who keep so many open.